CW00869831

Arts and Crafts to Art Deco

The Jewellery and Silver of
H.G. Murphy

Bunty –

Arts and Crafts to Art Deco

The Jewellery and Silver of
H.G. Murphy

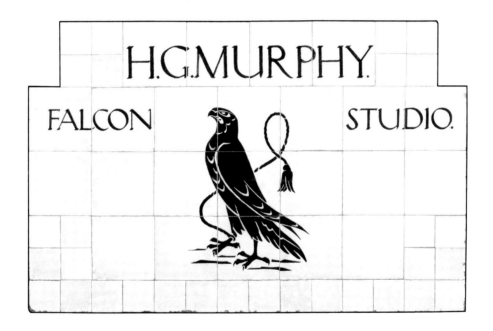

with good wishes

Paul Atterbury and John Benjamin

ANTIQUE COLLECTORS' CLUB

ISBN 1 85149 488 X

British Library Cataloguing-in-Publication Data
A catalogue record for this book is available from the British Library

Printed in China
for the Antique Collectors' Club Ltd., Woodbridge, Suffolk

FRONTISPIECE: *Studio portrait of H.G. Murphy, 1925*
TITLE PAGE: *Tiled shop board for the Falcon Studio, 1930s*

Antique Collectors' Club

Formed in 1966, the Antique Collectors' Club is now a world-renowned publisher of top quality books for the collector. It also publishes the only independently-run monthly antiques magazine, *Antique Collecting*, which rose quickly from humble beginnings to a network of worldwide subscribers.

The magazine, whose motto is *For Collectors-By Collectors-About Collecting*, is aimed at collectors interested in widening their knowledge of antiques both by increasing their awareness of quality and by discussion of the factors influencing prices.

Subscription to Antique Collecting is open to anyone interested in antiques and subscribers receive ten issues a year. Well-illustrated articles deal with practical aspects of collecting and provide numerous tips on prices, features of value, investment potential, fakes and forgeries. Offers of related books at special reduced prices are also available only to subscribers.

In response to the enormous demand for information on 'what to pay', ACC introduced in 1968 the famous price guide series. The first title, *The Price Guide to Antique Furniture* (since renamed *British Antique Furniture: Price Guide and Reasons for Values*), is still in constant demand. Since those pioneering days, ACC has gone from strength to strength, publishing many of today's standard works of reference on all things antique and collectable, from *Tiaras* to *20th Century Ceramic Designers in Britain*.

Not only has ACC continued to cater strongly for its original audience, it has also branched out to produce excellent titles on many subjects including art reference, architecture, garden design, gardens, and textiles. All ACC's publications are available through bookshops worldwide and a catalogue is available free of charge from the addresses below.

For further information please contact:

ANTIQUE COLLECTORS' CLUB

www.antique-acc.com

Sandy Lane, Old Martlesham
Woodbridge, Suffolk IP12 4SD, UK
Tel: 01394 389950 Fax: 01394 389999
Email: info@antique-acc.com
or
Eastworks, 116 Pleasant Street – Suite #60B
Easthampton, MA01027, USA
Tel: (413) 529-0861 Fax: (413) 529-0862
Email: info@antiquecc.com

FOR PAT CRACKNELL AND IN MEMORY OF BRIAN MURPHY

CONTENTS

Acknowledgements

This book, born out of a shared enthusiasm for the work of H.G.Murphy, simply could not have been devised or written without the complete cooperation and unwavering help of Harry Murphy's own family.

We should like to extend our special thanks and deep gratitude to Pat Cracknell who, apart from allowing us full and unrestricted access to all the family records, letters and archive material, also offered us a unique insight into the life and career of her parents, Harry and Jessie Murphy.

We are particularly in the debt of Shelagh Herbert and Gill Cracknell for giving up so much of their valuable time in the complex task of researching their grand-father's life and work. We should also like to extend our appreciation and thanks to Martin Herbert for his unflagging help and good humour over several visits. Elisabeth, Katherine and Susan Murphy gave us free access to the collection of the late Brian Murphy, while Rosemary Cracknell and Jessica Cracknell-Bowser should be mentioned for their own contribution.

The authors wish to thank Paul Dyson of the Goldsmiths' Company for organising the first major retrospective exhibition of H.G. Murphy's life and work while David Beasley gave us access to the Murphy material in the library at Goldsmiths' Hall and generously supplied us with photographs.

The following institutions or individuals kindly arranged for the loan of images or loaned images for the book: Dr Elizabeth Goring at the National Museum of Scotland; Dr Emmanuel Minne at the Royal Society of British Sculptors; Reverend Canon Gavin Kirk at Lincoln Cathedral; Dr Rex Colwell at All Saints Church, Evesham; Ann Ducker and Hylda Hopper at St Cuthbert's Church, Darlington; Vivien Gainsborough Foot at St Mary the Virgin Church, St Mary's Platt; Colonel A.W. Blackett OB.E. and Rob Cowie at Edinburgh Academy; John Carrie at Southern Counties A.S.A; Brian Pickard at United Hospitals Sailing Club; Mr and Mrs Ian Aldridge; David Church; Anthony Grey; Mrs A. Hemming; Judith Howard; Judy Payne; Kevin Quin, Dr Joseph Sataloff, Colin Turner and Louise Turner. Many people offered scholarly help and support, and shared their knowledge of H.G. Murphy and the Falcon Studio: Ann Eatwell and Eric Turner of the Victoria & Albert Museum, Margaretta Frederick of the Delaware Art Museum, Mark Golding, Andrew Morgan and J.G. Day of the Kandahar Skiing Club, Mary Greensted, Sonya and David Newall-Smith of the Tadema Gallery. Anita Anderson, David Callaghan, Paul Hollis, Eric Knowles and Charlie Major made extremely valuable contributions to broaden our understanding of Murphy's work.

We are particularly grateful to our photographer, Richard Valencia, for his professionalism and stoicism during several long and complicated sessions. Our thanks also to Don Wood for earlier photography of selected items of jewellery Photographs were also supplied by Christian Baur and Chris Jeffrey L.R.P.S. Unless stated otherwise, photographs of work by H.G .Murphy included in this book are from private collections.

Finally, the preparation of the text and the scanning of the artwork could not have been completed in such a short time without the tireless support and hard work of Chrissie Atterbury and Patricia Benjamin. We are indeed fortunate.

Paul Atterbury
January 2005

John Benjamin

Introduction

With a reputation second to none during his lifetime, Harry Murphy was arguably Britain's most versatile and innovative jewellery designer of the first half of the twentieth century, and one of the most influential silversmiths of the Art Deco era. His friends, supporters and clients included major figures from the worlds of art, craft, design and education, for example Sir Edwin Lutyens, Eric Gill, Henry Wilson, Frank Pick, Harold Stabler and Percy Jowett. One of the first to be nominated Royal Designer for Industry, the first Master of the RDI faculty, and Principal of the Central School of Arts and Crafts, Murphy was a widely revered figure who seemed in his many skills to encapsulate that early twentieth century dream, the successful marriage of art and industry. Yet, today he is little known.

Many modern jewellery historians barely acknowledge his existence, although Graham Hughes discusses his career in *Modern Jewelry: An International Survey* providing four illustrations of his most inspired work. He is not mentioned in the standard histories of the Arts and Crafts Movement written by Gillian Naylor and Isabelle Anscombe. He is overlooked by David Bennett and Daniela Mascetti in their celebrated work *Understanding Jewellery*. Shirley Bury gives him a passing reference as an assistant of Henry Wilson. Charlotte Gere and Geoffrey Munn give him a short, and rather dismissive paragraph in *Pre-Raphaelite to Arts & Crafts Jewellery:* '…Harry Murphy, originally employed in Henry Wilson's workshop as an errand boy, and whose silver designs show the greatest affinity with the geometric French work of the period. Murphy was

On 15 March 1938 Murphy made a television broadcast, from Alexandra Palace, discussing the role of the craftsman in industry with Leslie Mitchell, an event that reflected his standing at the time.

One of a series of twelve 1993 publicity posters in which the Victoria and Albert Museum publicised its own permanent collection. The use of Murphy's award-winning 1933 tea service (see page 82) on a V & A poster underlined his standing as a modernist, even though few people had heard of him at this time.

the living proof that Pugin's ironical joke about the office boy who designed in his spare time was not so absurd as he believed'. The errand boy story is echoed by Natasha Kuzmanovic in her biography of John Paul Cooper, who also quotes Cooper as saying: 'I had proposed Harry Murphy for membership (of the Arts and Crafts Exhibition Society) as being a good craftsman, not a designer'.

As a silversmith he has fared slightly better and his work has been included in a number of books and exhibitions about Art Deco and early twentieth century design. In his lifetime he exhibited widely, from regular appearances at the displays of the Arts and Crafts Exhibition Society to major international exhibitions. He won a gold medal at Milan in 1933, showed ten pieces at the

Paris Exhibition of 1937 and was an important exhibitor at British Art in Industry, held at the Royal Academy in 1935. One of his major supporters has always been the Goldsmiths' Company, of which he was a liveryman for many years, and his work has regularly been included in exhibitions of modern silver held at Goldsmiths' Hall, with notable examples in 1938 and 1965. He also featured extensively in *Treasures of the 20th Century*, the Goldsmiths' Hall millennium catalogue. Important examples of his work are in the collection of the Victoria & Albert Museum, but these were mostly only acquired in the 1980s, coincident with the appearance of work by Murphy in the salerooms and the antiques trade.

Henry George Murphy was born in Kent in 1884, the son of a groom and coachman. Having displayed an early enthusiasm for art and craft, he was apprenticed to Henry Wilson in 1899 and quickly became a key member of Wilson's studio, with specialist knowledge of enamelling and gold and silver work. By 1906 he was teaching at the Royal College of Art, and a few years later at the Central School of Arts and Crafts. In 1912 he opened his first London workshop, while continuing his association with Wilson and his teaching. In 1914 he married, and in 1915 joined the Royal Naval Air Service and trained as a seaplane pilot. Following his demobilisation in 1919, he pursued a variety of activities in the silver and jewellery trade through the 1920s, and then opened the Falcon Studio, a new workshop and retail outlet in Marylebone, London in 1928.

From this point his career took off, and from his workshop came a prodigious output of jewellery and silver, including domestic ware of all kinds, and commissions from civic, corporate and institutional clients, along with ecclesiastical work and sporting trophies. Everything made at the Falcon Studio was marked by the same distinction in design and finish. Brought up as he was in the traditions of the Arts and Crafts Movement, Murphy was above all a craftsman. However, unlike many of his contemporaries, he was able to combine traditional attitudes with a commitment to modern design, matched by a belief in the need to improve the standing of the

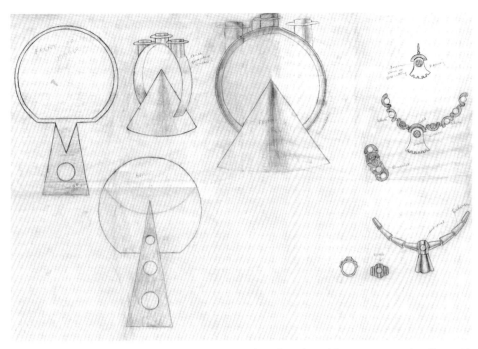

Sketches by Murphy for a modernist hand mirror and candlestick, and for contemporary jewellery with Egyptian and Inca influences.

silversmith. To his complete technical command of all kinds of metalwork, Murphy added a fine taste in design, giving by subtle changes a contemporary flavour to traditional forms and techniques. His beliefs, and his vision, led him to run a large workshop and a retail outlet, something that put him apart from his contemporaries and rivals such as Omar Ramsden, John Paul Cooper and Harold Stabler. In this he revealed his long enthusiasm for, and dependence upon, European attitudes to design and manufacture. His influences were French, German and, above all else, Scandinavian silversmiths, making him a powerful adherent of international modernism and Art Deco styling. As a result, he was involved in organisations promoting the cause of art and industry, such as the Design and Industries Association, and was friends with design luminaries such as Frank Pick. In 1938 Murphy was one of the first to be appointed Royal Designer for Industry.

Murphy was also throughout his lifetime a dedicated teacher. In 1932 he became Head of Silversmithing at the Central, and four years later he was appointed Principal of the School. He always devoted himself to the training of students, apprentices and young craftsmen in his industry. He also took an active interest in the efforts made by the Goldsmiths' Company to raise the standard of design in the trade.

At the height of his powers, influence and reputation, Murphy died unexpectedly in July 1939, a revered and much loved figure whose loss was widely felt, and expressed. In hindsight, this was the worst possible time for an artist and designer to die. Two months later came the outbreak of the Second World War and, when peace finally returned in 1945, everything had changed. Art Deco and international modernism had gone, Arts and Crafts attitudes had turned into history, and the 1930s fixation with marrying together art and industry seemed increasingly irrelevant. Silver and jewellery design and manufacture, now in the hands of many people who had been trained by Murphy, was swept into the turmoil of the Festival of Britain and 1950s style. Harry Murphy was simply forgotten.

This book, and its accompanying exhibition at Goldsmiths' Hall, will bring him back to life, and put him in place once again as Britain's most creative and imaginative jeweller and silversmith of the Art Deco era.

Unmounted enamel plaques found at the Falcon Studio after Murphy's death, some of which may date back to his time with Henry Wilson before the First World War

CHAPTER 1

Biography

Henry George Murphy, familiarly known as Harry throughout his life, was born in Birchington-on-Sea, Kent, on 27 October 1884. Perhaps significantly, in the light of future developments, the cottage in which he was born had previously belonged to Dante Gabriel Rossetti, who had died in 1882.

His father, Henry, by trade a groom and coachman, had married Mary Hamlin in Birchington in 1882. Henry was the second of four children, William, born in 1883, Nellie in 1886 and Jack in 1888. Harry's best friend from childhood was Frank Mann, who later married his sister Nellie. Frank, later a motor engineer, may have fired Harry's early enthusiasm for all things mechanical.

After the premature death of Harry's father in the early 1890s, the family moved to London, taking up residence at 2 Vine Terrace, Holland Street, Kensington. Harry attended the Fox School in Kensington Church Street and quickly revealed creative talents. It is recorded that he saved his pocket money to buy tickets to concerts at the Albert Hall, within walking distance of the family house

If ever there were a formative moment in Harry Murphy's career, it happened in 1894 when the ten-year-old boy, passing by chance the

Murphy with his mother, an uncle and his sister Nellie, in about 1916

Henry Wilson, c.1910

hall where the Arts and Crafts Exhibition Society's show was being set up, looked in through the open door. His interest attracted the attention of a tall, aesthetic-looking man who invited him in. This was the first meeting between Harry and his subsequent teacher and mentor, Henry Wilson, possibly the greatest British jeweller and goldsmith of his generation. Intrigued by the boy's obvious enthusiasm for the work on display, Wilson introduced him to both William Morris and Walter Crane, who were present in the room. It is said that Harry's conversation with Morris changed the course of his life.

This early exposure to the philosophies of the Arts and Crafts Movement was to have a profound effect. From this point, Harry devoted himself to education and self-improvement.

From this accidental meeting a friendship bloomed between Wilson and the Murphy family, ultimately resulting in Wilson asking permission from Mary Murphy to take the boy

Henry Wilson's workshop at his house at St Mary's Platt, Kent, c.1908. Left to right: Ernest Smith, a modeller and sculptor, Charles Baker, Henry Broun Morrison, Murphy, Sidney Wiseman

This Indenture Witnesseth, that *Henry George Murphy*

of *2 Vine Terrace. Holland Street. Kensington*

in the *County* of *London*

of h*is* own free will and accord, and by and with the consent and approbation
of his *mother* testified by h*is* executing these Presents, doth put h*im*self
Apprentice to *H Wilson*

of *17. Vicarage Gate. Kensington*
in the *County* of *London*
to learn the Art, Trade or Business of *silversmith and jeweller*

and to be with h*im* after the manner of an Apprentice from the *first*
day of *June* One thousand eight hundred and ninety-*nine*.
until the full end and term of *six* years from thence next following
and fully to be complete and ended ; during which time the said Apprentice h*is*
M*aster* faithfully shall serve, h*is* secrets keep, and h*is* lawful commands
obey ; he shall do no damage to h*is* said M*aster* or h*is* goods, nor suffer
it to be done by others, but shall forthwith give notice to h*is* said M*aster* of
the same when necessary ;— he shall not waste the said goods, nor lend them
unlawfully, nor shall he do any act whereby h*is* said M*aster* may sustain any
loss with h*is* own goods or others during the said term ; he shall not buy nor sell during
h*is* Apprenticeship, nor absent h*im*self from h*is* said M*aster* service day or night
unlawfully ; but in all things as a faithful Apprentice shall behave h*im*self towards h*is*
said M*aster* and others during the said term.

*and the said H Wilson doth hereby undertake to pay the
said Henry George Murphy a his services the following sums:
the first year five shillings per week. the second year
seven shillings the third year & fourth year nine shillings the
fifth eleven shillings and the sixth thirteen shillings.*

And the said *H Wilson shall teach instruct or cause* h*is* *to be taught and
instructed* said Apprentice in the Art, Trade or Business of *silversmithing & jewellery*
by the best means in h*is* power ~~shall teach and instruct or cause to be taught and instructed~~

~~The said~~

~~finding the said Apprentice sufficient Meat, Drink, Lodging and all other necessaries during~~
~~the said term~~

And for the true performance of all and every the said Covenants and Agreements the said
Parties bind themselves by these Presents IN WITNESS whereof they have to this
Indenture interchangeably set their Hands and Seals the *14th* day of *September*
in the year of our Lord One thousand eight hundred and ninet*y nine*.

SIGNED, SEALED and delivered)

Henry George Murphy.

Mary Ann Murphy.

H Wilson

in the presence of

Arthur Grove.

*I have much pleasure in certifying
that Mary M...ph... his ... & his
conduct is entirely ... satisfactory
in every way.
H Wilson*

The indenture for Henry George Murphy's six-year apprenticeship to Henry Wilson, drawn up on 14 September 1899

A typical multi-media production of the Henry Wilson workshop, indicating the diversity of metalworking skills that Murphy would have acquired during his apprenticeship and his subsequent years with Wilson. A number of Wilson pieces were probably made by Murphy and Wilson's other major assistants

Murphy teaching a silversmithing class, perhaps at the Central School of Arts and Crafts, in the 1920s

out of school. On 14 September 1899 Henry George Murphy was formally apprenticed for six years to Henry Wilson and, aged fourteen, he started work at Wilson's workshop at 17 Vicarage Gate, Kensington, a stone's throw from his home. Later he was to return to Kent, working at Wilson's studio at his home at St Mary's Platt, near Sevenoaks.

Henry Wilson (1864–1934) was initially trained as an architect. After completing his articles, he became chief assistant to J.D. Sedding, and completed projects left unfinished at Sedding's death in 1891. Sedding's premises were situated next door to Morris and Company's showrooms. Wilson's interest in metalwork started in about 1890 and he set up his own workshop in 1891 and employed, among others, John Paul Cooper and Bernard Instone, teaching them the basics of jewellery and silver design and construction. Wilson joined the Art Workers' Guild in 1892, becoming Master in 1917. A dedicated and selfless teacher, he worked at the Central School of Arts and Crafts from 1896 and at the Royal College of Art from 1901.

Encouraged by Wilson, already an established teacher there, Harry enrolled as a student at the Central School of Arts and Crafts in 1904. This was the start of a lifelong association with this institution, then at the peak of its reputation and authority in the field of applied arts. The Central had been founded in 1896, with George Frampton and W.R. Lethaby as joint principals. At this point, Lethaby, the leading polymath in the field of applied design, would have had a considerable influence upon the young Murphy. In 1908 and 1909 he was awarded first prize and silver and bronze medals in the City and Guilds examinations in goldsmithing.

While still a student, Murphy had started to teach, joining the staff at the Royal College of Art. He was to continue there until 1911, underlining not just his technical abilities but also his commitment to education. In 1907 the Prince of Wales, on a visit to the Royal College, congratulated Murphy on his work and 'gave him a warm handshake'. Throughout his adult life his exceptional teaching skills matched by a

Harry and Jessie, at the time of their engagement, c.1911

deep reservoir of enthusiasm made him highly regarded throughout the profession and in the community at large. In 1912, after leaving the Royal College, he joined the staff at the Central School of Arts and Crafts. He was employed initially to teach goldsmithing, jewellery and enamelling, working ten hours a week on Wednesdays and Fridays, at the rate of 30s. (£1.50) per attendance.

His apprenticeship ended in 1905. Clearly, his relationship with Wilson changed from this point, Murphy becoming much more a colleague and partner than a student. For a start, Wilson arranged for Murphy to teach at the Royal College. More important, there is a blending of the boundaries of authorship in the pieces coming from the Wilson workshop. Naturally pieces were credited to Wilson, as principal of the workshop. However, it is sometimes difficult to distinguish the work of Wilson from that of John Paul Cooper or Harry Murphy. Indeed, family

GOLDSCHMIED
E. LETTRÉ.

LADET ERGEBENST ZUR
BESICHTIGUNG SEINER
WERKSTATT EIN

UNTER DEN LINDEN 71

B E R L I N

HARRY G. MURPHY,
GOLDSMITH, ENAMELLER &
ARTISTIC METAL-WORKER
41, KEMPSFORD GARDENS,
E A R L S   ::   ::   C O U R T.

To _____ 191_

From _____

HARRY G. MURPHY,
GOLDSMITH, ENAMELLER &
ARTISTIC METAL-WORKER.
5, KENTON STREET,
RUSSELL SQUARE, W.C.

Publicity leaflet issued by Emil Lettré from his workshop in Berlin, c.1912

Murphy stationery from the Kempsford Gardens and Kenton Street workshops, 1912-14

records suggest that several important commissions conventionally attributed to Wilson were made by Murphy and others to Wilson's designs. This harmonious and symbiotic relationship was to continue on a formal basis until 1912, and informally until Wilson's death in 1934. A practical reflection of this was Murphy's decision to move back to Kent in 1910, when he took up residence in Whatcote Cottages, very close to Wilson's home and studio.

The move to Kent was also to change his personal circumstances. In 1910 he met Jessie Church, a teacher at a local school, and they were soon engaged, an event commemorated by a ring he made specially for her.

The impact of Arts and Crafts attitudes was international. In many places, for example in Scandinavia, it took the form of a revival of national and local traditions, as in the work of Jensen. In Austria the adherents of the Wiener Werkstätte were more enthusiastic about geometric and abstract design, anticipating the linear and architectural forms of Art Deco. In Germany, as in Britain, the emphasis was on craft studios and co-operative working practices, but with a greater enthusiasm for traditional styles which echoed the fervent nationalism of the era. Awareness of the many facets and styles of the Arts and Crafts Movement was facilitated by the series of international exhibitions and by the increasing number of magazines and publications, such as *The Studio*. At some point, Wilson had come in contact with Emil Lettré, an established German jeweller and silversmith working in Berlin. Wilson must have told Lettré about Murphy's precocious talent, for it is recorded that Lettré tried to persuade Wilson to encourage Murphy to move to Germany. By this time, Murphy must have been aware that he needed a wider horizon. In the spring of 1912, after Wilson had left Britain for an extended stay in Venice, to execute sculpture in bronze, Murphy, now in effect a free agent, accepted the post of foreman at Lettré's workshop in Unter

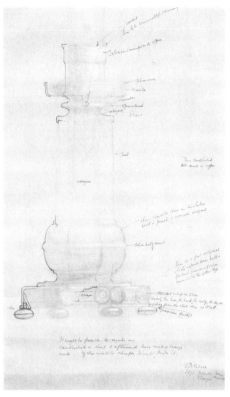

Signed design for a copper candlestick by Henry Wilson, sent by Wilson from Venice to Murphy in 1913, with detailed instructions for its manufacture

den Linden. Significantly, Bernard Instone, another Wilson protégé, was already ensconced with Lettré in Berlin.

A number of factors were to make this a difficult chapter in Murphy's life. Firstly, there was a disagreement between Murphy and Lettré about the starting date for the job. Murphy, always a plain-speaking and intensely loyal man, made it clear to Lettré that he could not break his contract and leave the Central before the end of the academic year in June 1912. Lettré, on the other hand, expected him to come as soon as the employment had been agreed. Secondly, it is likely that Instone, already well established in the workshop, cannot have been thrilled about the imminent arrival of a former studio colleague as his foreman. In the event, Murphy started work in Berlin on 7 July 1912, taking up lodgings with Instone at Knaustrasse 12, Berlin-Friedenau. Almost daily letters between Harry and Jessie at this time reveal his loneliness, homesickness and the steady deterioration in the working

relationship with Lettré. The workshop was extremely busy, and the hours were as a result long and arduous. The letters show that Lettré, while highly competent, was peremptory and inclined to bad temper. The situation was compounded by the uncomfortable relationship with Instone. On 24 August, just forty-eight days after arriving in Berlin, and presumably following a heated exchange of views, Murphy was sacked by Lettré, who questioned his professional integrity and skill. This caused Murphy to seek redress from the British Consul, to no avail, and he was quickly back in Britain.

In the autumn of 1912 Murphy, determined now to stand on his own feet, took premises at 41 Kempsford Gardens, Earls Court, in West London. Success appears to have been immediate and sufficient work came in for him to employ an apprentice, aged fourteen, 'a smart lad who did well'. In November 1913 he moved to larger premises at 5 Kenton Street, Russell Square, taken on because of the close proximity to the Central School of Arts and Crafts, and within a year was employing ten people. His reputation was clearly

Pair of candlesticks made by Murphy from the Wilson design

spreading, for in September 1913 he was offered a job at Birmingham School of Art by Arthur Gaskin. He also received an approach from Ipswich School of Art. Despite all this, remarkably little is known about his work during this period and few pieces can be identified and dated with certainty. The only reference in family documents is to the design for the Knight Companionship Collar of the Most Illustrious Order of St Patrick in June 1913. In a letter to Jessie, Harry described this as: 'a tremendous piece of work' going on to say: 'I have had half a dozen other good commissions besides'. The implication of this is that by 1913 Murphy was well established as a jeweller, capable of fulfilling the most prestigious commissions for the upper echelons of society. His skills in enamelling, niello work and all aspects of jewellery making were well known, underlined by his increasing reputation as a teacher.

Inspired by the success of the business and his comfortable financial position, Murphy felt able to marry. Business income apart, he was also earning £200 a year from his teaching at the Central, an indication that his habit of taking on too much and working too hard was already established. By December 1913 he was discussing the building of a house in Kent with his architect

friend, Kingsley McDermott. On 19 August 1914, two weeks after the outbreak of the First World War, Harry and Jessie were married at St George's Church, Wrotham and they moved into their newly completed house, named Falhalla – pronounced feharler, and the Gaelic for 'a little green place'. Their marriage was the culmination of a long engagement, during which the relationship had been sustained during the periods of separation by the constant exchange of letters. Although the train journey to and from Kent took under an hour, Murphy frequently stayed in London to work late in the evenings. Many letters refer to the continual pressure of work and the money worries caused by the perennially slow payment of invoices. These letters give the first hint of stress–related illnesses, affecting his blood and his eyes.

The First World War had an immediate impact upon the luxury goods trades and so Murphy was quickly compelled to seek alternative kinds of employment for his staff.

On 2 December 1914 the Admiralty accepted his tender for the manufacture of 2,400 metal and enamel On War Service badges, at a cost of £22 per thousand, with 800 required within seven days. This was the first of a number of

Murphy, left, in his Kenton Street workshop, with unidentified assistants, in about 1913. Visible on the bench is the lion-handled London cup (see page 21) and in the background a pair of the Wilson-designed candlesticks

Studio photograph of Jessie at the time of her marriage in 1914. She is wearing the silver and gold pendant set with opals, made for her by Murphy in 1913, and shown in the adjacent photograph taken in August 1913. In the locket centre is the engagement photograph shown on page 17. See also page 43.

similar orders. While this kept the workshop in business, it was boring and repetitive, and deeply frustrating to a man of Murphy's creative ability. In 1915 he decided, therefore, to enlist in the services. In July he was released by the Central and in the same month he was passed out as a Leading Mechanic in the Royal Naval Air Service, based initially at Hendon. Through the period of war service he maintained his contact with Wilson, and with other colleagues. The workshop was closed up and unfortunately was

An early corporate commission for Murphy, a lion-handled City of London cup made in 1913 at Kenton Street

Murphy during his Royal Naval Air Service days, in his flying suit and in a seaplane cockpit, probably photographed at the Windermere base in about 1916

Souvenir brochure of the Cattewater seaplane station, produced in 1919, and signed by Murphy (top left) and fellow pilots, officers and colleagues

Chief Petty Officer Murphy with pilot instructors at speed on Lake Windermere in the motor launch Nacia, *in 1916 or 1917*

never to reopen due to the landlord having relet the premises at a much higher rent. By 1916 he was a qualified seaplane pilot, based at RNAS Windermere and in November he was promoted to Chief Petty Officer. Subsequently posted to the Scilly Isles, he finished the war at the Cattewater seaplane base near Plymouth. When the Royal Air Force was formed on 1 April 1918, Murphy was commissioned as an officer and he remained in the service until 1919.

The role of Jessie during this period was significant. From 1915 she ran what remained of the business, combining the roles of administrator and book-keeper and gaining experience that was to prove to be vital in the future. On 14 April 1917, their daughter Patricia Mary was born. Their son, Brian Robert, was born on 5 June 1920.

Murphy came back to an uncertain world. Although he returned to teaching at the Central, the workshop had been lost, money was in short supply and he spent considerably more time at home. Always a keen gardener and sportsman, he landscaped the grounds at Falhalla, creating a rockery, terrace, fruit orchard and, ultimately, a tennis court, using local labour. For the next few years he was something of a journeyman silversmith and jeweller while considering various business opportunities, including a partnership in a shop in Bond Street, a dealership in Paris and even a pharmacy shop in Kent. He also travelled, and in 1921 renewed his association with Germany, visiting Frankfurt, Leipzig and Dresden, as well as making trips to Prague and Geneva. He was back in Germany again in 1924, visiting Hanau-am-Main, a centre of metalwork production. Also in 1924 was his involvement with the Royal Doll's House project for Queen Mary, making miniature versions of the Crown Jewels as well as tiny copies of gem-set gold and silver jewellery. The completed Doll's House was shown at the Wembley British Empire Exhibition in 1924. Perhaps as a result of this, Murphy was later awarded his most important

Family life at Falhalla during the 1920s. Top, the house with Patricia and Brian in the still undeveloped garden; centre, some years later with the family car; bottom, relaxing in the garden

Murphy approached most things in life with verve and determination, including mowing the lawn

Falhalla was always a kind of animal and bird sanctuary. This is Pete, one of the many family pets

commission, a jewelled tiara for the Princess Royal.

In 1920 he had been approached by J.P. Mitchell, the owner of a suite of offices and a lapidary workshop in Pall Mall East, and asked to become initially a consultant and later managing director of the London branch of the Sapphire Mining Company, an Australian enterprise. This expanding company later moved to larger premises in Kingsway, Holborn. Murphy set up and ran the London office and its associated gem-cutting rooms and controlled from London the output of the Australian mines. Much of the output was sold to wholesalers and manufacturing jewellers in France, involving Murphy in regular trips to Paris. He worked closely with Mitchell, and there was discussion about the opening of a retail shop in London, funded by Mitchell or the company. However, letters suggest that Murphy's relationship with Mitchell was uneasy and so his involvement with the enterprise was relatively short-lived.

In 1925 he acquired his first car, a Vulcan, registration AH 2097, and built a garage at home, where, as a trained mechanic, he carried out his own maintenance. His daughter remembers that he was always under the car. A sociable man, Murphy filled the weekends with picnics with friends, visits to the cinema in Maidstone or Tonbridge and, weather permitting, playing tennis and cricket, and going swimming. Trips to London included visits to Wimbledon and the Boat Race, the Hendon Air Pageant and outings to the British Museum, the Science Museum and the Queen's Hall. Holidays were often spent camping on the south coast, interspersed with a day at the races at Goodwood. The family remembers seeing the Schneider Trophy seaplane races in 1929. Animal life was always important and dogs, goats, hens, rabbits and geese filled the house and garden. The sequence of silver roundel brooches with animal and bird subjects echoes this aspect of family life and Murphy's enduring love of nature. Murphy was a man of diverse talents and restless imagination. It is, therefore, not surprising to find that in September 1928 he even patented a new type of expanding suitcase.

During this period the need for permanent, well-equipped premises became paramount. Work was still coming in and having to be carried out without his own workshop. It is possible he used the facilities at the Central, or even Wilson's studio in Kent. Finally, in 1928,

The likely inspiration for the Murphy falcon, a 17th century Mughal painting in the British Museum, and, below right, the Falcon Studio trademark, a woodcut by the engraver George Friend

buildings at the back, opening on to an enclosed yard. The ground floor was converted to house a polishing lathe, rollers, wire drawing bench and other heavy equipment. On the first floor there was a workshop area with a ten-place bench in the centre and a partitioned-off bedroom area. At the front there was a shop and office, under Jessie's supervision. Metal-framed Crittall windows painted oyster grey gave the shop a modern, uncluttered look and an interior resembling, according to Jessie, the inside of a jewel case. By now the business needed a name and so the Falcon Studio was born, along with the now familiar falcon rebus, designed by the engraver, George Friend. The inspiration for the name came from Jessie herself, a jess being the short strap of leather or silk used to secure the legs of a hawk on its stand or on the wrist. The falcon emblem was then used on the shop sign, on stationery, boxes and pouches and, most significantly, was registered as part of the hallmark used on silver and gold. The chosen livery for the studio was green and cream, even to the almost exclusive use of green ink for invoices and letters.

suitable premises were located at 58 Weymouth Street, Marylebone. The building, a former chemist's shop, was eminently suitable in that it could allow for noxious fumes, noise and even the presence of an acid bath, basic requirements for the jewellery and silver trade. However, the key attraction was the extensive range of

H. G. MURPHY
CRAFTSMAN IN FINE METALS
GOLDSMITHING, SILVERSMITHING
ENAMELLING AND ENGRAVING
HERALDRY
58 WEYMOUTH STREET
PORTLAND PLACE
LONDON, W.
TELEPHONE : WELBECK 9400

Murphy's trade card for the Weymouth Street workshop, showing the use of Friend's falcon design

The Falcon Studio, either Weymouth Street or Marylebone High Street, 1930s

Hallmarks used by H.G. Murphy and the Falcon Studio from 1928

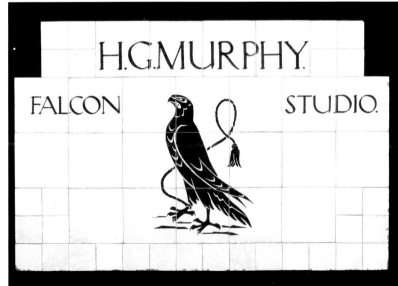

Punches, stamps, jewellery bags and the tiled shop board for the Falcon Studio, all featuring the familiar falcon trademark

The work bench at the Falcon Studio, probably Marylebone High Street, late 1930s

This concern for detail reflects the contemporary enthusiasm among many companies, large and small, for a definable corporate identity.

It was the combination of a large dedicated workshop with retail premises in the heart of London that separated Murphy from the vast majority of his contemporaries and put him on a par with long-established names such as Jensen and Tiffany. This courageous approach brought quick and lucrative rewards. The Falcon Studio flourished immediately, with a host of commissions received from institutions, livery companies, civic authorities, churches and sporting associations, along with the day-to-day activity of a busy retail shop selling directly to the public. In 1929 Murphy was elected a Freeman of the Goldsmiths' Company and of the City of

London and in 1930 to the Art Workers' Guild. The next year he was admitted on livery to Court at Goldsmiths' Hall.

Murphy was now a fully established figure. As well as running the business and teaching, his work encompassed trade fairs, conferences and committees. As his workload increased and reputation broadened, conversely the world entered a period of financial decline, the direct result of the 1929 Wall Street crash. By 1931 he wrote that 'the shop & workshop are empty'. Cash flow problems intensified, made worse by domestic demands such as school fees, bills and rent. His health suffered accordingly. In another letter he said he was seriously considering taking a job. Accordingly, on 31 March 1932 he applied for the position of Head of Silversmithing at the

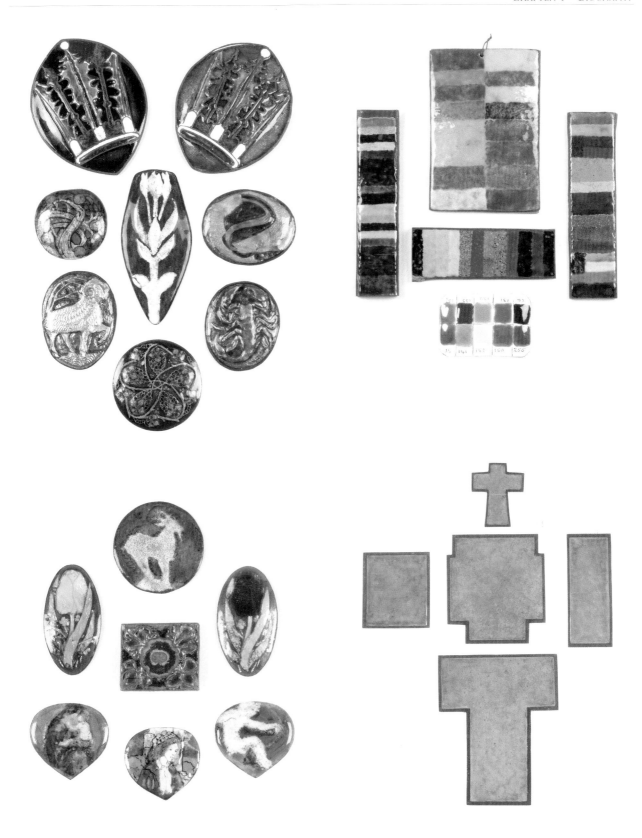

Enamel plaques and enamel colour test panels, from the stock of unused pieces found at the Falcon Studio after Murphy's death in 1939. Some of these will date back to Murphy's apprenticeship and the era of Henry Wilson, before the First World War

Diploma that accompanied the award to H.G. Murphy of a gold medal at the Milan International Exhibition of 1933. For a photograph of the teaset that achieved the award, see page 82

Central School of Arts and Crafts. His referees were Henry Wilson, Sir Edwin Lutyens, Alfred Turner, Harold Stabler and F.V. Burridge (a colleague at the Central). He was successful in this application. By now he and Lutyens were friends, their association probably dating from the Royal Doll's House commission.

Ironically, as he took on his new job and considerable extra responsibility at the Central, the trade began to recover. As a result, the pressures on him increased.

Interestingly, he had by now re-established harmonious relations with Emil Lettré, whom he had met at a jewellery congress in London in 1931. Lettré now clearly regarded him as an equal and their new found friendship was to continue until Murphy's death.

From 1932 the work built up again and commissions rolled in. This was the start of a highly productive period, working in tandem with other important silversmiths and craftsmen such as Professor Richard Gleadowe, the engraver, George Friend and Eric Gill. Loyal customers of the Falcon Studio included Frank Pick, John Betjeman, Lutyens, Hugh Dent, the son of the

publisher J.M. Dent, and the composer Sorabji.

This period was also defined by a significant change in style, particularly in the field of silver-smithing, with a new emphasis on line engraving and the modernist and geometric forms of Art Deco, far removed from the historicist and traditional techniques of the Arts and Crafts Movement. This new style manifested itself in a greatly increased range of domestic silver and jewellery, designed to capture the taste of the moment. At the same time, major commissions resulted in the production of a series of fine sporting trophies and decorative and functional wares in a modern idiom for churches, livery companies, institutions such as the Royal Institute of British Architects and the Royal Society of Arts, and private companies. At this time the design and manufacture of sporting trophies was actively encouraged by competitions organised by the Goldsmiths' Company.

Murphy also exhibited the products of the Falcon Studio with increasing frequency, though usually under his own name. His display at the Milan International Exhibition of 1933 won him a gold medal and he also showed at the international exhibition in Paris in 1937. On a more domestic scale he was a regular exhibitor at the Arts and Crafts Exhibition Society, an organisation of which he was president, and the Red Rose Guild in Manchester, and was represented at the Dorland Hall exhibition of 1933 and the Exhibition of British Art in Industry, held at the Royal Academy early in 1935. Despite this, Murphy still suffered desperately from cash flow problems and at one point his overdraft had reached £950. It seems that his business abilities did not match either his creative skill or his reputation. It is likely that he undercharged to keep the workshop busy and that the resultant narrow profit margins were quickly turned into losses by long delays in payment.

As before in 1932, these money problems may have encouraged Murphy to apply for a job. In this case it was the post of Principal of the Central School of Arts and Crafts, replacing the recently retired William Augustus Stewart. His application was supported by testimonials from F.V. Burridge, Sir Edwin Lutyens, Noel

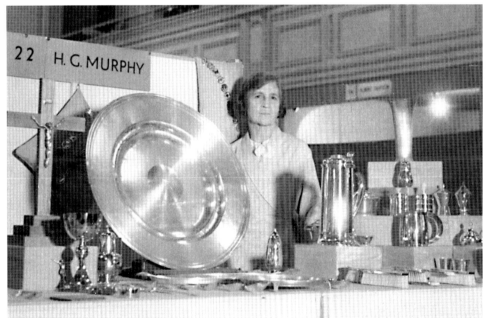

Displays of Murphy silver and jewellery in the mid-1930s, at the Red Rose Guild in Manchester. A number of pieces illustrated in this book can be identified, along with the massive alms dish shown by Murphy in Berlin in 1938

Jessie and her daughter Pat looking at a display of Murphy pieces at an exhibition in the late 1930s

A contemporary catalogue photograph showing examples of Murphy silver displayed at the British Art in Industry Exhibition, held at the Royal Academy in London in 1935. All these pieces were loaned by the Worshipful Company of Goldsmiths

Carrington, Arthur Wakeley and G. Yeo of Wakeley & Wheeler, the publisher Hugh Dent, the silversmith J.B. Harrison, Lawrence Tanner, Clerk to the Weavers' Company, the writer Herbert Maryon and William Read, a colleague from his time with Sapphire Mining. There were fifty-five applicants, but Murphy was selected from the final shortlist of three. It was a great personal triumph and the final accolade on a lifetime dedicated to teaching. On his appointment he received a large number of congratulatory letters from, among others, Harold Stabler and Frank Pick. The latter wrote: 'I only hope it will not withdraw you from the sphere of craftsmanship too much', a sentiment echoed by many who wrote to him on this occasion. Being Principal made huge demands upon Murphy, particularly at a time when his business was thriving. As a result, he simply worked harder and tried to fit more into each day. Frequently he stayed in London after working late and, as was so often the case, sustained his relationship with his family by writing long letters on a daily basis. Apart from his teaching, and the administration of the Central, he was now called upon frequently to give lectures to colleges, learned societies and

The Goldsmiths' Company study group at the Paris International Exhibition of 1937, led by Murphy, in the centre of the photograph

professional bodies about the techniques of his craft, about the position in society of the jeweller and silversmith and about the status of the artist and designer in industry, a subject on which he held strong views. On occasion the lectures were accompanied by images projected from specially-made glass slides.

In 1935 he was invited by the government of the Irish Free State to reorganise Irish Crafts Schools and to rebuild the gold and silver-smiths crafts in that country.

Money may also have played a part in the decision to move from Weymouth Street, although equally important was the imminent redevelopment of the area for residential purposes. In this new environment noxious fumes and noise would certainly have been out of place. New premises were finally found nearby, at 22 Marylebone High Street, and in 1935 the Falcon Studio was re-established there, along with its retail shop. The rent was £60 per annum. As ever a vital support for her husband, Jessie commuted daily from Borough Green to run the showroom and office and to organise exhibition displays.

RÉPUBLIQUE FRANÇAISE
MINISTÈRE DU COMMERCE ET DE L'INDUSTRIE

EXPOSITION INTERNATIONALE
DES ARTS ET DES TECHNIQUES

PARIS
1937

DIPLOME COMMÉMORATIF

DÉCERNÉ À M. G. Murphy London
Classe 44. Sélection Nationale Britannique
Le Commissaire Général,

Murphy's diploma awarded at the Paris Exhibition in 1937

In the latter part of the 1930s Murphy was a frequent visitor to Germany. In 1935 he attended the Jewellers' Congress in Berlin, was invited on to international committees and visited Pforzheim and Stuttgart. The following year he travelled to Brussels, Munich and Berlin, where he took part in an international exhibition of

H. G. MURPHY
CRAFTSMAN IN FINE METALS.

FALCON STUDIO

22, MARYLEBONE HIGH ST.
LONDON, W.1

———

GOLDSMITHING. SILVERSMITHING.
ENAMELLING AND ENGRAVING.
HERALDRY.

Telephone : WELBECK 9400.

HAND WROUGHT
JEWELLERY
CUPS
BOWLS
SPOONS
TEA AND COFFEE SETS
ECCLESIASTICAL WORK
CHALICES
CIBORIA
CROSSES
PRECIOUS STONES
PEARLS
EMERALDS
RUBIES
SAPPHIRES
OPALS
Valuations for Probate and Insurance
Old Gold and Jewellery Bought
Jewellery Remodelled
Repairs   Restringing

Trade card from the Falcon Studio at 22 Marylebone High Street, indicating the range of work undertaken

silver and crafts. He wrote to Jessie: 'The exhibition is very good and stimulating, the Danish silver is by far the best. The Italian pavilion is the most disturbing it is terribly original, strong, full of vitality and at the same time full of destruction, it is the most dominating note of the exhibition'. He also attended the Olympic Games, held in Berlin in 1936, staying with Emil Lettré. He transmitted his excitement in a letter to Jessie: 'I am feeling really fine. On Sunday Lettré took me to one of the most important families in Berlin very wealthy and they entertain all the important people who come to Germany…it was a small party, several

Olympic champions were there and later the marathon runners passed the bottom of the garden so we had a fine view near the finish…I am going to the art exhibition and in the afternoon to see some fencing. In the evening Lettré is entertaining the English polo team.'

The next visit to Berlin was in 1938, for the great international craft exhibition organised by the Nazi government. Murphy won a gold medal for his display, and was featured in local newspapers. While clearly excited by Germany and German design, Murphy seems to have been less than impressed by the Nazis. On a postcard to Jessie he described one parade as a 'grotesque

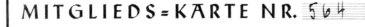

MITGLIEDS=KARTE NR. 564

für Herrn H. G. Murphy, London

DEUTSCHE GESELLSCHAFT FÜR
GOLDSCHMIEDEKUNST E. V.

DAS PRÄSIDIUM:

Ludwig Roselius   R. Krohne   F. R. Wilm
       Paul Hamel   Bruno E. Werner

GESCHÄFTSSTELLE: BERLIN, JERUSALEMER STRASSE 25

1936

Murphy's membership card for the international jewellery congress held in Berlin in 1936

Murphy in Berlin in 1936, with German colleagues

spectacle' and in a letter written from the Hotel Kaiserhof he ended: 'The chauffeur has just called for me...he is complete with military uniform and clicks and salutes like a tap dancer.'

On this visit Murphy was accompanied by his friend George Hughes, the Assistant Clerk of the Goldsmiths' Company and one of the most significant supporters of Murphy and the Falcon Studio. It was Hughes who was instrumental in setting up some of the important exhibitions held at Goldsmiths' Hall in the 1930s, notably those devoted to imported luxuries in 1932 and to modern silver in 1938. He ensured that Murphy was well represented in the latter. That same year, Murphy was called to the Court of Assistants of the Goldsmiths' Company.

In many ways 1938 was Murphy's *annus mirabilis.* On 25 February he attended a celebration at the Royal Society of Arts to receive the award of Diploma of Royal Designer for Industry from the Duke of Gloucester. This was the first presentation of the new award, which entitled the holders to use the initials RDI after their name. Murphy was in exalted company, receiving his diploma with Douglas Cockerell, Eric Gill, James Hogan, J.H. Mason, Keith Murray, Tom Purvis, Harold Stabler, Fred Taylor, C.F.A. Voysey, E. McKnight Kauffer and the representatives of the late George Sheringham. In addition, Murphy was appointed the first Master of the RDI Faculty.

The RDI scheme had been planned some time before, and the recipients were sworn to secrecy. Murphy heard about it in October 1936 and wrote to Jessie accordingly, in a typically self-deprecating manner: 'The degree is not a degree, it is a new Diploma the Royal Society of Arts have instituted for distinguished designers in industry...don't talk too much about it and I don't want it to appear in the papers. I haven't had time to accept it yet. Don't overdo the boosting of HGM it has a boomerang tendency and too much becomes harmful you have

Murphy displaying the alms dish included in his display at the international crafts exhibition in Berlin in 1938. This photograph appeared in German newspapers at the time

Medals awarded to Murphy for his City and Guilds qualifications in 1908 and 1909, along with others awarded in Germany in the 1930s

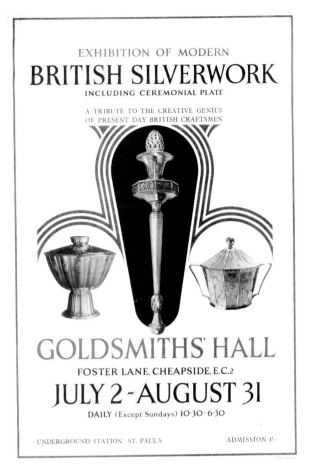

The poster for the British Silverwork exhibition held at Goldsmiths' Hall in 1938, organised by George Hughes. The piece on the right was made by Murphy

no idea how these things spread and I don't want any misunderstanding of my character. I am not out for popularity, my job of work is too serious for that sort of thing.'

During the latter part of 1938 Murphy's health began to deteriorate, a decline provoked by years of overwork and living a stress-filled life. Despite this, he continued to work at his usual rate, and many fine pieces emerged from the Falcon Studio bearing hallmarks for 1938 and 1939. His last major commission, destined to be unfulfilled, was probably the supervision of the design and production of the extensive range of church plate for the new Guildford cathedral, a project that he was addressing with his usual enthusiasm, underlined by his friendship with Edward Maufe, the Cathedral architect. Unable to relax, he continued to overexert himself, with the result that his various ailments turned into a serious illness. His last completed work was probably a bronze plaque for the National Association of Boys' Clubs, mentioned in an article in *The Builder* in July 1939. Harry Murphy died on 10 July 1939, aged fifty-four.

A TRIBUTE BY P. H. JOWETT

TO THE MEMORY OF

HENRY G. MURPHY

PRINCIPAL OF THE LONDON

COUNTY COUNCIL CENTRAL

SCHOOL OF ARTS & CRAFTS

MCMXXXVI TO MCMXXXIX

WHO PASSED AWAY AT THE

MASONIC HOSPITAL LONDON

ON THE TENTH DAY OF JULY

IN THE YEAR MCMXXXIX

Tribute booklet designed and printed by Leonard Jay at the Birmingham College of Arts and Crafts and issued after the memorial service held for Henry G. Murphy at St Michael's, Cornhill, London on 17 July 1939

Murphy's death provoked a genuine and widely felt sense of loss among friends, clients, colleagues and students, many of whom expressed surprise at its suddenness. There were a number of obituaries and published reminiscences, some serious and some light-hearted, linked by the common desire to capture not just the achievement but also the character of a man clearly seen to be remarkable. One newspaper wrote: 'A most jolly and jovial man – his vast laugh could be heard ringing through the school – he was greatly beloved by his pupils, and entered enthusiastically into their schemes.' *The Times,* while taking care to reflect generously upon his career and his standing as a leading silversmith and designer, was also concerned to express his personality: 'But it was for his personality as much as for his work as an artist that he will be remembered. It is a sad thought that one's first recollection of Murphy is striding across a room filled with students, radiating health and optimism. His great laugh, direct and fearless outlook, and his insight, which cut through pettiness and hypocrisy, will never be forgotten by his friends or his enemies. A characteristic reply to some tentative scheme was "Yes, I'm all for it," and one knew that one had an ally to the end. By members of the Court of the Goldsmiths' Company he will be remembered as one of the great silversmiths in a long line of great names.'

Jessie also received a large number of letters of condolence, from professional associates, colleagues and friends. These were generous in their praise, and united in their sense of loss. Harold Stabler, who had been taught by Murphy at the Royal College of Art, called him: 'the greatest silversmith of his time'.

E.M. Rich, Education Officer for the LCC, wrote: 'his death is a great blow to industrial art education'. Omar Ramsden referred to: 'the high esteem in which he was held' and similar sentiments were expressed by Bernard Instone. Professor Gleadowe wrote: 'It is hard to realise that one can count no more in this world on his sympathy and courage and energy and loyalty…I shall miss him more than I can say as a friend and fellow worker.' For Edward Maufe, the loss was of both a 'charming friend…and staunch supporter in the work of Guildford cathedral'. Lord Sempill, President of the Design and Industries Association called him: 'the British Cellini'. The designer, Reco Capey, writing on behalf of the Arts and Crafts Exhibition Society, of which Murphy was President, said: 'Your husband was loved by all who knew him – the Society has lost its moving force – and I have lost a dear friend'.

A memorial service for Murphy was held at St Michael's, Cornhill on 17 July 1939. Among the many present were the great names of art, craft, design and education. The address was given by Percy Jowett, a friend and colleague, and an equally dedicated educationalist.

His words sum up the man:

Let us thank God for the life and example of His servant Henry George Murphy:

For his skill as a craftsman,
For his inspiration as a teacher,
For his vision and appreciation of beautiful things,
For his courage and unselfishness,
For his undaunted optimism and enjoyment of life,
For his humanity and understanding of men.

Colourful naturalism observed in designs for a necklace and two rings, c.1930.

CHAPTER 2

Jewellery

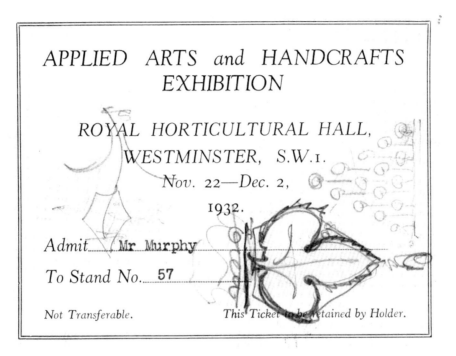

APPLIED ARTS *and* HANDCRAFTS
EXHIBITION

ROYAL HORTICULTURAL HALL,
WESTMINSTER, S.W.1.
Nov. 22—*Dec.* 2,
1932.

Admit Mr Murphy

To Stand No. 57

Not Transferable.   This Ticket to be retained by Holder.

Murphy's preliminary sketch for a naturalistic pendant; a good example of Murphy's creative imagination rarely, if ever, at rest

Harry Murphy's very existence as both artist craftsman and commercial jeweller would have been far less meaningful if prevailing fashions at the end of the Victorian Age and beginning of the twentieth century had been rather different.

To gain an understanding of just how much repetitive and unimaginative jewellery was pumped out for the masses in this golden era, all one has to do is to inspect the windows of antique jewellery shops or the pages of auction catalogues today. The typical 'turn of the century' ring would be set with a cluster or hoop of diamonds and colourful gems such as ruby or sapphire while the use of cheap and robust nine carat gold resulted in a mass of whimsical and decorative little pendants, brooches, chains and bracelets set with a variety of inexpensive semi-precious gems – garnet, aquamarine, opal, peridot and pearl – in designs which could hardly be described as innovative or ground-breaking. For customers with only a few shillings to spare, the workshops in Birmingham churned out cloyingly sentimental silver brooches depicting symbols of good luck and friendship such as horseshoes, swallows and shamrocks while sweetheart brooches depicting popular girls' names – Ada, Florrie, Hilda and Ivy – spread through the country like an unstoppable rash.

At the same time, the recently discovered diamond mines situated at Kimberley in South Africa were servicing the needs of a burgeoning and confident British middle class. Jewellery shops the length and breadth of the country sold

A group of Falcon Studio miscellanea; antique pinchbeck watchcocks converted into jewels and subsequently plated; naturalistic silver plaques made into jewellery or the finial of a spoon and two silken book marks with silver plaque finials

diamond star brooches, crescent brooches and flower sprays or, if clients were sufficiently wealthy and socially well connected, diamond necklaces, earrings and tiaras. In 1895, one London jeweller was able to supply its customers with diamond rivières – necklaces of diamonds in graduated formation – in no fewer than *twenty-three* different sizes.

In such a climate of mass production and mechanical output it was perhaps unsurprising that a sense of revulsion grew in certain sections of society appalled by the gross superficiality of all this repetitive industrialisation. Throughout the country small groups of artisans and isolated craftsmen coalesced to form workshops, societies and guilds in which the old skills of metalworking, enamelling, engraving, setting and polishing could be be practised and learnt anew.

In the 1880s and 1890s several schools of art, guilds and societies were founded to foster and nurture the talents of these passionate craftsmen. In 1884 the Art Workers' Guild was established in

Early studies including two satsuma ware brooches, two abalone shell brooches, a carved jadeite plaque fashioned in silver as a pendant and pearl trefoil earrings in leaf cluster frames

London to promote the cause of the embryonic Arts and Crafts Movement while in 1887 the Arts and Crafts Exhibition Society offered a showcase for members of the Guild to display their work. In 1888 Charles Robert Ashbee founded the Guild of Handicraft in London in which individual designers worked in an atmosphere of creative harmony and mutual co-operation. Two years later the Birmingham Guild of Handicraft was established by Arthur Dixon on much the same lines as its London counterpart. In 1901 the Artificers' Guild was set up in Chiswick by Nelson Dawson and Edward Spencer and soon became a potent location in London for several leading designers to meet and exchange ideas.

Many of the chief exponents of their art started off their careers in unconnected professions such

as architecture and teaching but the Arts and Crafts Movement gave them the opportunity to change direction and develop their talents in the media of goldsmithing, silversmithing and metalwork. It was in this vibrant atmosphere of creativity that Henry George Murphy was to thrive, gaining his skills from one of the greatest of all English artist craftsmen – Henry Wilson.

Wilson established his first workshop in 1891 employing, amongst others, John Paul Cooper to learn the technical skills of metalwork, goldsmithing and silversmithing. In 1899 he took on a fourteen-year-old boy called Harry Murphy to learn the rudiments of the business. It quickly became apparent that, in spite of his youth, Harry Murphy displayed a rare and precocious talent. It should be borne in mind that Murphy received a very rudimentary education before joining Wilson's workshop and it is thus a testament to Wilson's kindness and great ability as a teacher, as much as to Murphy's intuitive brain and desire to better himself, that the boy progressed so rapidly in the workshop environment.

Wilson's decorative output was greatly influenced by Gothic and Renaissance art and design. This resulted in bold, structural jewellery complemented by bright primary colours of enamel in designs which exhibited a strong tendency towards religious symbolism – Virgin and Child, Angels, Deities and the Crucifixion – fashioned in architectural frames reminiscent of seventeenth century 'tabernacle' pendants. Sailing ships and castles evoked a sense of Arthurian heroism and chivalry while nature and naturalism, surely the greatest inspirations for all artist craftsmen, were beautifully articulated in gold pendants and necklaces depicting flowers, trees, birds and rivers. Beyond Wilson's wonderfully sensitive imagination lay the ability of a highly able metalworker supremely competent in the methods and application of many of the fundamental skills of the silversmith and goldsmith. These included repoussé work, hammer work, soldering, carving, embossing, moulding and polishing as well as the complex technical procedure involved in enamelling glass to precious metals. Wilson, ever the teacher and a man

willing to share his knowledge with all, incorporated all this mass of information in his celebrated book *Silverwork and Jewellery,* first published in 1903.

Henry Wilson was an inspiration to all who came within his sphere and he clearly had a profound influence on the creative output of many designer craftsmen active at the time and, most particularly, the work of Cooper and Murphy. Several decorative motifs such as leaf sprays, beading and wirework are common to all. Both Wilson and Cooper leant heavily on religious and medieval iconography including angels, galleons and castles while Murphy's application of intricate and colourful enamelling is virtually indistinguishable from Wilson's own and there has been much debate regarding attribution ever since. Since Murphy worked at the same bench as Wilson, it is highly likely that master invited apprentice to finish enamel, engrave settings and mount gems. Indeed this was the artist craftsman's creed – a sharing of knowledge, teaching methodology and instilling good working practice. It was to be the guiding principle throughout Murphy's own life; several of his own important silver commissions, for example, were designed by Richard Gleadowe and engraved by George Friend – the perfect example of skilled and dedicated craftsmen working together in an atmosphere of mutual respect and productive harmony.

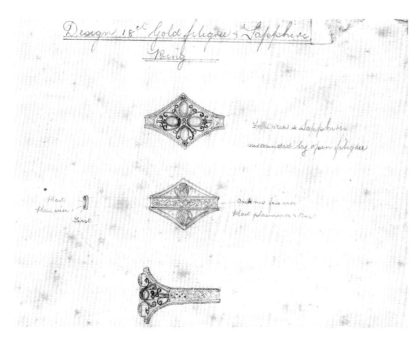

An early design for a gold filigree ring exhibiting Murphy's meticulous skill as a draughtsman

Silver and gem-set earrings and Jessie Murphy's naturalistic opal and silver pendant with central locket compartment containing a photograph of Harry and Jessie

Murphy, The Creative Perfectionist

As much as Harry Murphy was an idealistic artist craftsman, he was also a retail jeweller, silversmith and metalworker running a shop in the centre of London combining the burden of manufacturing and selling with the personal responsibilities of teacher, lecturer, husband and father. In this, he differed fundamentally from the vast majority of his contemporaries who, although highly accomplished craftsmen and women, lacked the necessary acumen and desire to run a profitable retail business. Not that Murphy ever actually made a significant amount of money in spite of his prodigious output; customers could be highly demanding but were often alarmingly slow in paying for their purchases – if they ever paid at all

– and it is clear that cash flow was sometimes rather precarious. Fortunately, Murphy could always rely on his redoubtable wife and business partner Jessie to look after the accounting side of the business and chase debtors. It should thus never be underestimated just how critical Jessie Murphy was to the success of the Falcon Studio.

Although a number of Murphy's working diagrams and watercolour sketches are dated, particularly those executed in the 1930s, the vast majority of his early designs bear no such inscription. Correctly judging a precise chronological sequence is therefore difficult. Murphy favoured the use of colourful enamel throughout his career while strong Arts and Crafts naturalistic themes such as trees, flowers, leaves and scrolls are found in a large number of pieces designed as late as 1932. It is only the later Art Deco pieces, strongly commercial and frequently repetitive, which can be accurately dated from the early 1930s to 1939, the year of his death.

Murphy probably started to design and make simple pieces of silver jewellery in around 1900 while serving his apprenticeship with Henry Wilson. These early examples included brooches, cufflinks and tiepins of simple geometric shape

One of Harry Murphy's earliest works – a silver and polychrome enamel plaque brooch, c. 1905

Early brooches and pendants including a simple niello bar brooch in a later Falcon Studio box

Apprentice pieces in silver and niello and later dress studs

'Medieval' gem-set pendant, probably an early workshop piece c.1910-1915

A polished garnet bead in a gold cagework frame, almost primitive in its simplicity

THE WORSHIPFUL COMPANY OF GOLDSMITHS

Multi gem-set pendant and matching necklace probably made in Wilson's studio, whereabouts now unknown

Design for a Gothic pendant together with (right) the completed necklace and pendant illustrated with an assortment of 'Medieval' and 'Celtic' jewels executed in around 1910

often decorated with niello. Murphy became something of an expert in the use of this subtle form of ornamentation contributing a chapter on the subject in later editions of Wilson's *Silverwork and Jewellery* (see Appendix 2).

Some of the earliest examples of Murphy's work are illustrated together on a card which forms part of the family archives. Decidedly medieval in design, several of the pieces are decorated with niello and are set with an assortment of polished gemstones. These include a large circular 'Celtic' silver brooch with an etched design of woodland nymphs, a seal pendant, a gem-set plaque engraved with the design of a saint and two rectangular silver and niello brooches probably awarded as prizes at the Royal College of Arts Fancy Dress

Ball. A watercolour exists of the most elaborate piece in the group: a necklace of torpedo-shaped beads, possibly glass or enamel, suspending at the centre a Gothic quatrefoil pendant bearing the impression of a standing figure in a frame of four polished gem beads, probably amethyst or garnet, with a series of emerald and blister pearl drops suspended below.

By 1905 Murphy had completed his six-year apprenticeship with Henry Wilson and for the next five years he worked as a fully fledged craftsman in Wilson's studio. This was a period of intense activity and creativity spent perfecting the technical skills of the goldsmith, silversmith and metalworker. By this time he would have gained a high level of competence as an enameller and

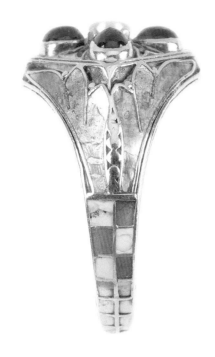

A bold, architectural champlevé enamel, emerald and diamond 'skyscraper' ring c.1930. See also the group of rings illustrated on page 64

Left and above: The betrothal ring made by Harry Murphy for Jessie Church in 1910. Note the green and white checkerboard enamelling on the shank – something of a Murphy trademark

would have been taught the methods involved in every conceivable aspect of the craftsman's art from how to shape the bowl of a spoon to making a fleur-de-lis motif on a gold pendant.

In 1910 he left Wilson's studio and spent the next year as an itinerant journeyman gaining experience in several workshops. His reputation was clearly growing because in 1912 he was persuaded to travel abroad to Germany where he was offered the post of foreman working with Emil Lettré, an eminent Berlin goldsmith and manufacturer. Lettré came from a Huguenot

Although Murphy used the Falcon Studio motif in the majority of his rings, many brooches and pendants revealed no such identifying marks. The enamel and gold roundel brooch is unusual for exhibiting not only the Falcon rebus but also the monogram 'HGM' and the applied mark '18 ct.'

Design for an early 1930s colourful gem-set enamelled gold 'tree' brooch (top left) together with a preliminary pencil drawing and watercolour of a cloisonné enamel, opal and diamond 'mushroom' brooch. The finished article is shown at bottom right

family of goldsmiths who had settled in Hanau in around 1600. In spite of a difficult childhood, he persevered with his studies and opened up a workshop in Berlin in 1900. In 1907 he received an important commission to design and make a silver service on the occasion of the marriage of Crown Prince Wilhelm to Cecilie von Mecklenburg-Schwerin. Now fully established in a workshop in Unter den Linden, he employed a large team of craftsmen making artistic jewellery and silver. His knowledge and appreciation of

Arts and Crafts no doubt brought Murphy to his notice and there must have appeared to be great potential in the relationship. Sadly, this was not to be. Lettré proved to be a demanding and unpredictable employer who worked his staff relentlessly. Although there were periods of enjoyment, particularly at weekends, Murphy felt desperately homesick and unhappy as his letters to Jessie clearly testify. Nevertheless, his time in Berlin was instructive and introduced him to a new set of working practices which would give

A splendidly intricate water sapphire cabochon, gold and gem-set pendant exhibiting Murphy's technical prowess in the medium of enamel. Note the interesting entwined geometric strapwork motifs and the application of unusual cream-coloured enamel

him invaluable experience when running his own retail business. He would have also seen at first hand many of the fresh and innovative designs of the German Jugendstil Movement.

After returning to England in the autumn of 1912, business began to prosper, allowing Murphy to establish premises in London. In August 1914, after a four year engagement, he married Jessie Church at St George's Church, Wrotham, Kent. Naturally, Harry made Jessie's engagement ring, a gold hoop with quatrefoil-shaped bezel set with a half pearl in a cluster of four cabochon sapphires. The mount, decidedly Gothic in design, is enamelled in red, green and blue extending to the inner hoop of the ring itself which was inscribed and dated 1910. This

ring, together with a large number of Murphy jewels, was stolen some years ago but was subsequently recovered although, regrettably, the original inscription in the betrothal ring had been crudely scraped away.

Murphy was highly proficient in the techniques of enamelling and was accomplished in its application to any number of media. As previously discussed, his style was remarkably similar to Wilson's, even to the use of bright, bold colours – reds, blues and greens – which bring to mind the jewels of the Renaissance era. Pendants, necklaces and brooches were either decorated with *champlevé* enamel in which the surface of the chosen metal was cut away to create shallow individual cells which were filled with powdered enamel, fired and levelled smooth, or *cloisonné* enamel where wirework *cloisons* are soldered to the surface of the metal, filled with enamel and then fired. An excellent example of the former technique is an 'architectural' gold, emerald and diamond ring in which the *champlevé* enamel decoration is reminiscent of a New York skyscraper while a curious brooch fashioned in the shape of a mushroom is *cloisonné* enamelled in blue, brown, black and cream studded with opal and diamonds. The original watercolour sketches

and line drawings, still with their accompanying silver wirework *cloisons,* are retained in the Falcon Studio archive. One of the finest examples of Murphy's enamel work is the circular gold pendant mounted with a pale blue water sapphire in a highly complex frame decorated with a ring of cream, green and violet enamel in turn surrounded by a series of five emerald and enamel conical sections with elliptical crossover motifs set with rubies in between. Characteristically, the back of the pendant is just as

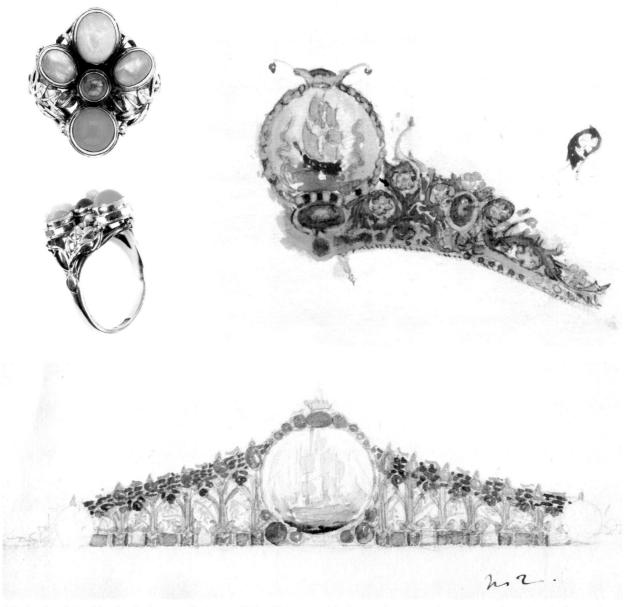

The head and shoulder detail of a naturalistic enamelled gold ring set with three opals, a green chrysoprase and a ruby cabochon and two watercolour designs for a jewelled tiara. The lower example contains elements of the 'Princess Royal' tiara illustrated opposite

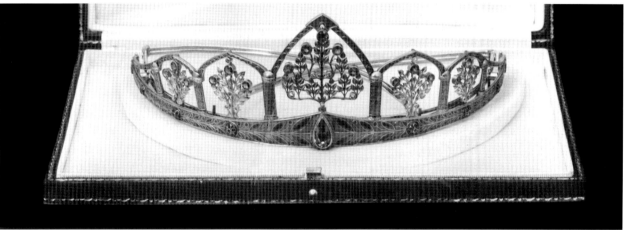

Pencil, black ink and gold leaf study for a tiara together with the original photograph showing the finished work in its fitted case. This photograph bears an inscription that the tiara was 'designed and made by H G Murphy for Princess Royal'

The Princess Royal tiara

Watercolour and gold leaf design for a heart-shaped gold pendant together with the original photograph of the finished jewel in its fitted case

intricately worked as the front with its apricot enamel trefoils and checkerboard enamel edging.

The outbreak of war in 1914 had a profound effect on Murphy's creative energies and at the same time the steady flow of private commissions more or less dried up. The Kenton Street Workshop, now employing up to ten people, experienced a radical change in direction with the order from the War Office to make large numbers of Admiralty enamelled badges with the lettering 'On War Service'. The majority of these were fashioned in metal gilt and a small number

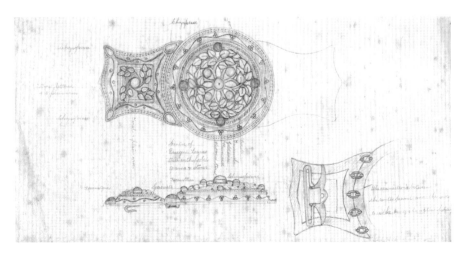

Left and opposite: One of Harry Murphy's most elegant creations, a silver and gem-set buckle with the designer's characteristic 'Tree of Life' motif

in silver. Jessie commented that the entire workforce hated this repetitive and mind-numbing undertaking and it is unsurprising to learn that Murphy threw it all up and joined the Royal Naval Air Service in 1915.

In around 1922 Murphy received one of his most significant commissions: a tiara in gold, enamel and gems to be worn by Mary, the Princess Royal, to mark the occasion of her betrothal to the Earl of Harewood. Considering the importance of this commission – by Royal Command from Queen Mary, the Princess Royal's mother – it is surprising just how little information exists in the Murphy family archive. It should also be said that the present Earl of Harewood does not recollect the piece in question. What there is extends to the original working diagram in black ink, pencil and gold leaf together with the black and white photograph of the completed tiara in its fitted case. This photograph is annotated on the back 'designed and made by H G Murphy for Princess Royal'. The tiara itself now forms part of a private collection in America where, perhaps unsurprisingly considering the striking comparisons, it has been attributed to Henry Wilson.

Fashioned as a series of Gothic arches in architectural formation, the framework is enamelled in blue and green with the design of simple foliate sprays decorated with apricot enamel buds and, at intervals, red enamel bosses. Contained within each arch is a 'Tree of Life' motif – Murphy's trademark device – each set with round-cut sapphires and brilliant-cut diamonds in cut-down millegrain collets. The lower gallery is set at the centre with a pear-shaped golden brown citrine and the pillar-like divisions and arches are further decorated with matching enamel highlights. The overall design of the piece contains elements of Henry Wilson's 'Diana' tiara of 1909 and Wilson's celebrated 'Orpheus' tiara presented by the Llewellyn Smith family to the Worshipful Company of Goldsmiths.

The 'Tree of Life' motif was used freely by Murphy in a wide variety of objects such as the handles of silver caddy spoons, paper knife finials, flatware and bowls as well as being incorporated in jewellery of greater complexity. The term for a tree representing the geneaology of Christ is known as a 'Jesse' – like the Falcon rebus a visual play on words which neatly weds Murphy's trademark design with Jessie's own name. Two of the most

Replicas of the Crown Jewels made for Queen Mary's Doll's House and exhibited at the British Empire Exhibition held at Wembley in 1924

elegant jewels are a heart-shaped gold pendant decorated with enamel, opals and pearls, of which only a watercolour and photograph now exist, and a splendid silver belt clasp studded with garnet, chrysoprase and moonstone cabochons which still survives in a private collection.

A fascinating aspect of Murphy's technical virtuosity was his ability to design and construct jewellery in miniature. He received from Windsor Castle the commission to make the miniature jewellery and associated regalia for Queen Mary's Doll's House which was due to be exhibited at the British Empire Exhibition to be held at Wembley in 1924. The objects included tiny replicas of the Imperial State Crown complete with enamel 'ermine', orbs, mace and sceptre and a group of miniature gold and silver brooches, bracelets, earrings and rings of which a replica set forms part of the family collection. To get some idea of the scale of one or two of the items, it is worth noting that the opal and gold bracelet is 45mm in length and the top of the turquoise ring is 5mm in diameter.

The move to busy West End premises in 1928 and Murphy's growing reputation as an accomplished goldsmith and silversmith inevitably resulted in a sharp rise in new business. The Falcon Studio now had to juggle the demands of large-scale commissions in silver for livery companies, church commissioners, sporting associations and civic institutions with the time-consuming demands of one-off rings, pendants and brooches for a disparate, and no

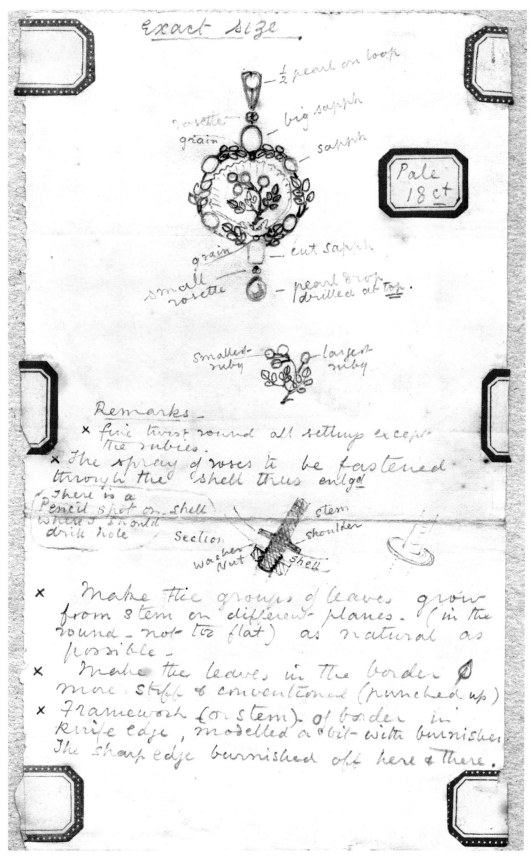

A design for a gem-set gold pendant offers a fascinating insight into the technical complexities involved in its construction

A collection of tiny gold, silver and gem-set doll's house miniatures in their original Falcon Studio case

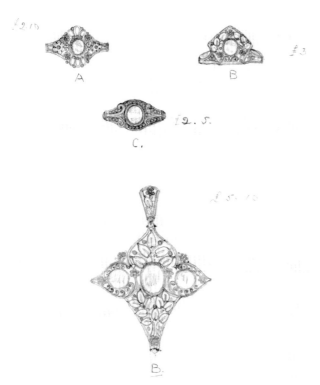

Early Falcon Studio designs for rings and a pendant. Bearing in mind the profit margins of many contemporary jewellery retailers today, Murphy's pricing structure can almost be seen as charitable.

doubt demanding, private clientele. Cash flow, however, continued to be precarious. It is interesting to note the cost of some of the jewellery which was being designed in around 1930. A fairly complicated ring in silver and gold set with a polished gem is priced at £3 or less while a gem-set pendant – heavily labour intensive – sells for £5.10s. Clearly, the execution of a quality hand-made object took precedence over commercial pragmatism.

By the late 1920s and very early 1930s, the fashion for strong blocks of colour and an altogether linear, architectural structure so characteristic of the Art Deco movement was fast superseding the softer, naturalistic forms of the Great War era. Harry Murphy, like so many craftsmen at that time, had to change direction quickly and embrace an altogether new and expressive style. The freshness and originality of his jewellery designs at this time are quite startling in their conception. While he still manages to retain his favoured natural forms such as leaves, trees and

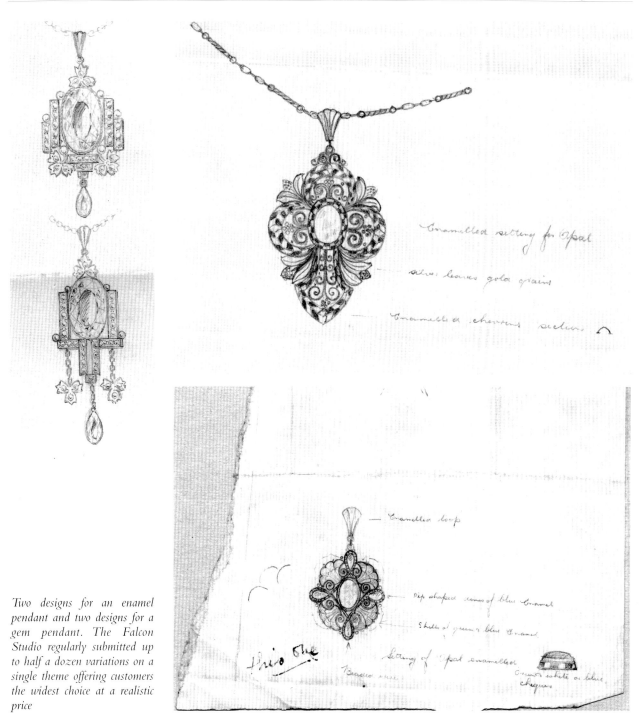

Two designs for an enamel pendant and two designs for a gem pendant. The Falcon Studio regularly submitted up to half a dozen variations on a single theme offering customers the widest choice at a realistic price

flowers, his confident and bold approach to rings, earrings and pendants reflects a strong influence of the Orient and even the dynamism of the *Ballet Russe*. This bold and daring look is thus demonstrated in a pair of splendid oxblood coral pendant earrings with bell-shaped enamelled gold cap surmounts and another similar pair with spindle-shaped lapis lazuli batons in green and red enamel mounts with matching fan-shaped finials. The design of a ring incorporates a diamond-shaped lozenge of coral in a calibré sapphire and emerald frame while a pendant set with primary coloured gems in stepped formation evokes all the extrovert confidence of the Jazz Age.

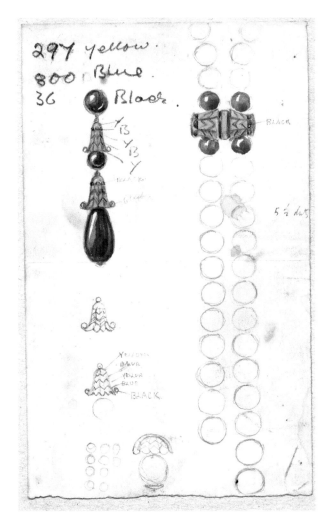

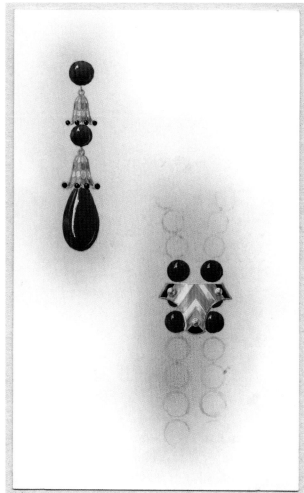

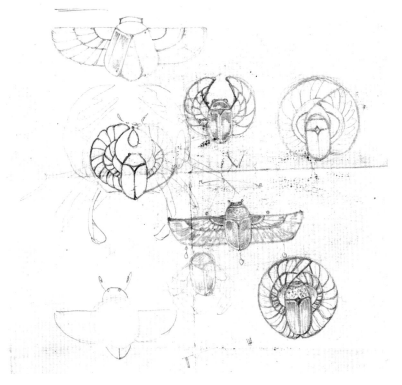

Two designs for ox-blood coral earrings with enamelled bell-shaped gold caps, with further designs for coral beads with enamelled clasps. The 'Egyptian scarab' brooch drawings reflect the universal appeal of Pharaohnic jewellery inspired by Carter's discovery of Tutankhamun's tomb in 1922

The pair of ox-blood coral, enamel and gold earrings (left) and the similar pair (below) mounted with lapis lazuli 'spindles' not only show that Murphy was designing jewellery of exceptional beauty and originality in the late 1920s and early 1930s but was also developing his own unique genre in one of the most creative periods of the 20th century

Oriental-style chrysoprase and gold ring decorated with scrolls and beading

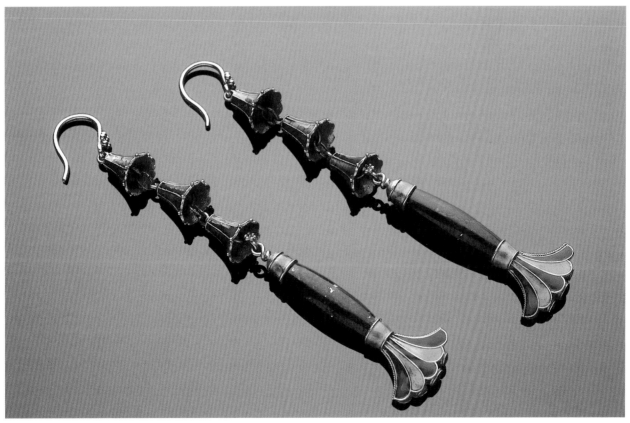

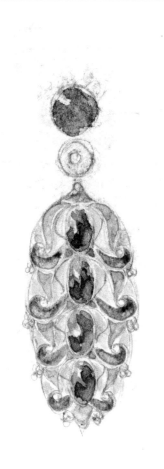

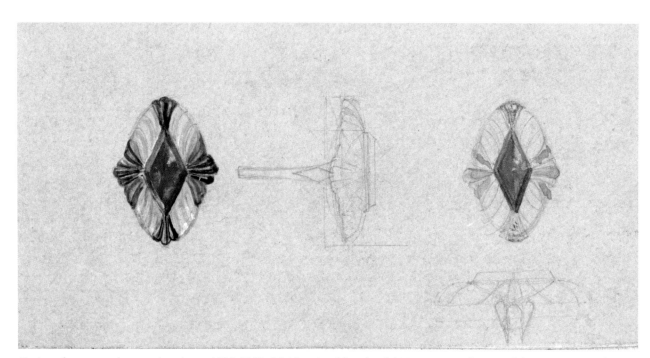

Designs for two pendants and a ring, c.1930-1932. Highly colourful and exhibiting strong influences of the Orient, Murphy was fascinated by the theatre and the exotic vibrancy of the Ballet Russe

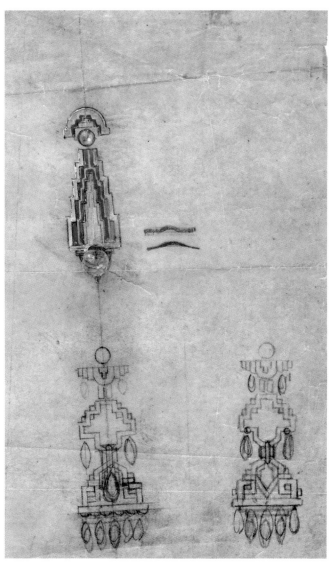

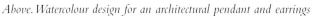

Above. Watercolour design for an architectural pendant and earrings

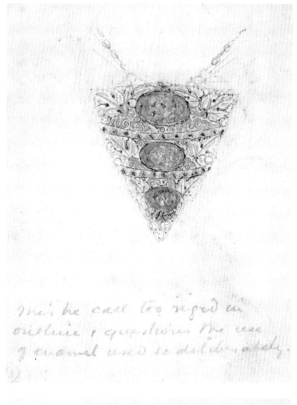

Top right. Design for a pyramid-shaped naturalistic pendant set with opals and decorated with enamel. Clearly not to the customer's exacting requirements

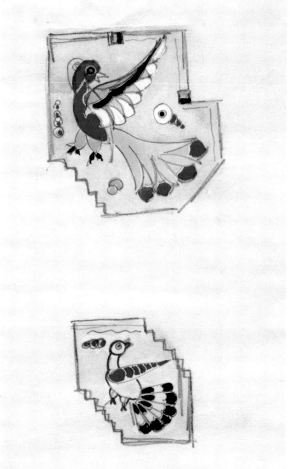

Right. Murphy's charming observations of birds, fish and animal subjects were captured in the Falcon Studio's range of silver figurative brooches (see page 67)

The Falcon Studio in the 1930s

The photograph of four silver, gem-set and hardstone pendants dated by Murphy himself in 1931 neatly shows a designer in transition. Aspects of the past include the use of Arts and Crafts gems such as rose quartz, turquoise matrix, coral and moonstone while the look of the future is anticipated in the bold fluted lines, the zigzag structures and the sheer architectural symmetry of the frames. Naturalism lingered until around 1932, as seen in a series of extremely pretty designs for a gem-set pendant with leaf and scrollwork decoration. By way of contrast, workshop diagrams also dated 1932 show the cool monochrome simplicity beloved of the international Art Deco jeweller. It is thus perfectly possible that Harry Murphy was by this time working in two parallel styles satisfying both the needs of his old established Arts and Crafts clientele and the requirements of an altogether newer and more sophisticated customer seeking cutting-edge modernism from a central London retailer.

After 1933 there is very little evidence of any of the softer, natural imagery being designed and the working drawings from 1935 until Murphy's death in 1939 exhibit a decidedly commercial look in which subtle variations on a theme would be submitted to the customer for selection. These include a rather dull and two-dimensional emerald and diamond plaque brooch, a diamond clip, a series of interesting designs for a large cabochon sapphire and gold ring and a black opal ring in no fewer than eight different varieties of architectural frame.

Four bold Falcon Studio silver, hardstone and gem-set pendants. This original photograph is dated 1931

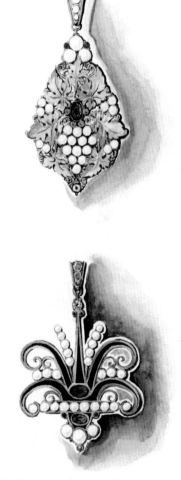

Falcon Studio designs for naturalistic pendants, c.1931

The bottom pendant on page 62 composed of a large faceted rock crystal drop in a silver frame set with coral, pearl and moonstone cabochons. The silver necklace interspaced with rock crystal and coral beads may not be original

NATIONAL MUSEUM OF SCOTLAND

Design for an architectural pendant with Olympic flaming torch symbol. By the mid-1930s naturalistic imagery had clearly given way to the clean, minimalist lines of Art Deco

Designed by H.G. Murphy
Falcon Studio

An advertisement for seven various diamond and gem-set rings illustrating the sheer diversity of Falcon Studio output in the 1930s. Note the 'skyscraper' ring (centre left) illustrated on page 47 and the 'Oriental' ring (centre top) illustrated on page 59

A group of three watercolours for early 1930s gold gem-set pendants of transitional design

Design for a pendant, c.1932. Murphy often favoured gems of irregular shape and natural form echoing his Arts and Crafts background.

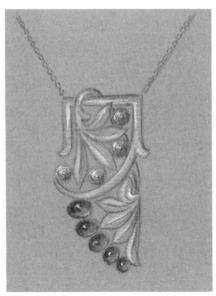

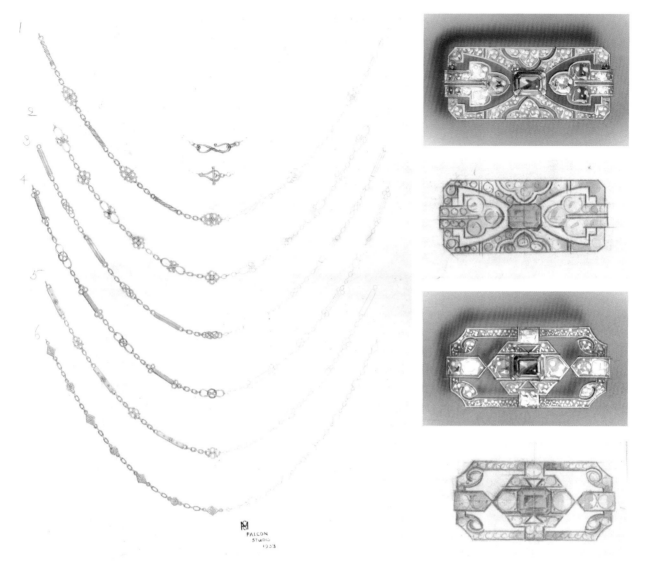

Variations on a theme: six designs for gold suspension chains

A group of sketches and watercolours for an emerald and diamond plaque brooch and an architectural pendant. By 1934 the demands of running a commercial business in the centre of London meant that the Falcon Studio was obliged to manufacture a range of designs which could only be described as repetitive and functional

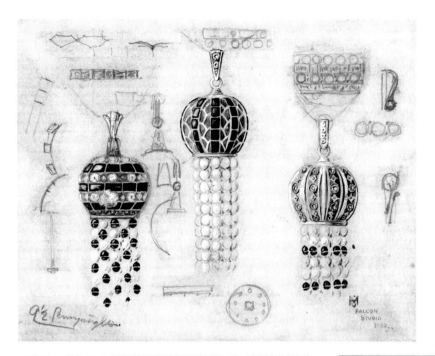

Design for a bracelet with enamelled bobbin and torpedo-shaped sections, three onyx, enamel, diamond and pearl tassel pendants and a significant commission – a large sapphire and diamond architectural pendant, c.1932-35

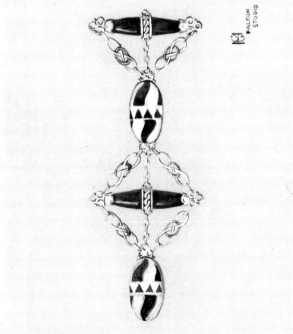

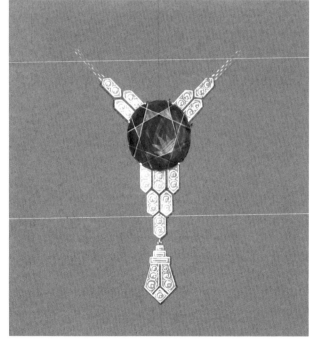

The Falcon Studio's Range of Silver Jewellery

Harry Murphy designed and made a large amount of inexpensive silver jewellery – he was, after all, primarily a silversmith completely at home in the medium. Among his most popular designs was a series of flat circular brooches based upon a number of interesting themes. The best known examples were the 'Signs of the Zodiac' range, each modelled in the craftsman's charmingly inimitable style. Animals and birds always appealed to both Harry and Jessie. Other menagerie subjects included a flamingo, a duck and a parrot as well as a series of designs based upon polar wildlife: an Arctic fox, an albatross, a polar bear and a whale. All these brooches sold in the 1930s for 12s.6d. and are highly wearable today.

Other examples of silver jewellery include bangles of classical inspiration, some of which were

The Falcon Studio's ever-popular range of figurative brooches including signs of the zodiac, animals, birds and even a Welsh leek. The hoop earrings are set with stained chalcedony cabochons

Silver jewellery was relatively easy to manufacture and many pieces were simple but extremely effective. The long guard chain (opposite) is mounted with cornelian cabochon sections in three-by-three formation while the ivory earrings (above) are similar to the ox-blood coral earrings illustrated on page 59

mounted with banded onyx, ivory or rose quartz; pendant earrings set with polished ivory beads in graduated formation (strongly similar to the ox-blood coral earrings previously discussed), bracelets composed of wavy plaques decorated with niello fish with bubbles coming out of their mouths, and rings sometimes mounted with bold and colourful hardstones such as malachite, agate or turquoise.

Harry Murphy was unquestionably an English Art Deco craftsman and nearly all the silverware and silver jewellery which he made in the 1930s exhibits one or more features of his abiding fascination for all things linear and architectural. A perfect example of his inimitable style is a silver ring in which the bezel is nothing more

A fine silver pectoral cross decorated with niello highlights in a frame of blister pearls

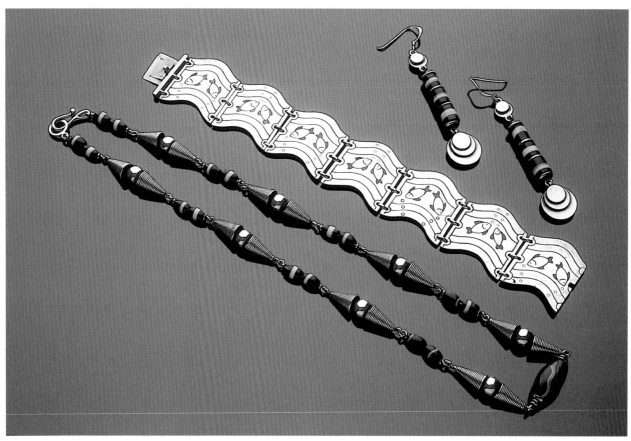

Banded onyx and silver necklace and pendant earrings together with an evocative silver wavy panel bracelet decorated with pairs of fish. Note the little air bubbles

Silver tablet ring with coiled tubular hoop and an azurite ring between stepped architectural shoulders

A pair of flat-cut silver pig earrings, inspired by a doodle drawn by Brian Murphy's teacher in 1935, together with a chiastolite and silver pendant with block suspension loop

than a plain, flat, oblong tablet measuring 20mm x 10mm. The sheer minimalism of this design is highly distinctive and extremely unusual, particularly as the tubular hoop of the ring is in contrast to the bezel decorated with a series of rope-like coils. A ring mounted with a cabochon of blue and green mottled azurite is set in an octagonal portrait frame flanked by multiple stepped shoulders, a feature repeated in a series of drawings for a ruby cabochon gentleman's signet ring. Another favourite motif used in earrings and necklaces involved a series of three or more graduated, overlapping discs fashioned on both sides of a silver rondel-shaped plaque while raised bars of the plainest possible design lent a cool severity to pendants, necklaces and, indeed, flatware. The influence of Scandinavian silversmiths such as Georg Jensen is clearly apparent here, particularly with Murphy's tendency to use polished hardstone cabochons such as green and blue chalcedony and cornelian to offset the rather unforgiving decoration on the silver mounts.

It is interesting to note that very few items fashioned in gold survive which are of comparable design to all this linear, minimalist output. It is almost as if Murphy allowed himself the luxury of using silver only for inexpensive experimental jewellery whilst gold was retained for more formal and commercially acceptable pieces appropriate for his retail market.

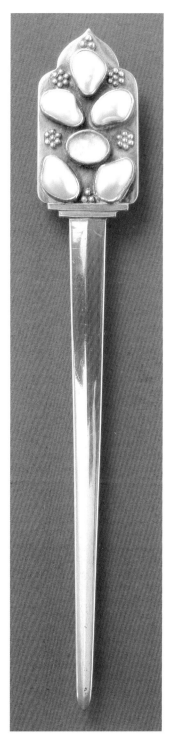

Long silver 'sword' brooch mounted with irregular pearls, a rock crystal cabochon and gold beading decoration

PRIVATE COLLECTION

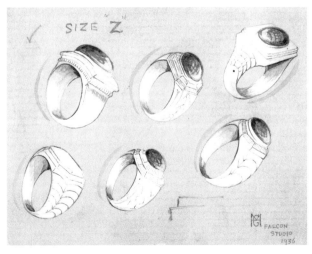

Six designs for a gentleman's ruby cabochon and platinum signet ring

Original photograph of a Falcon Studio suite of pendant, brooch, ring and earrings and (below) a similar set of opal, moonstone and silver jewellery with gold bead and lozenge highlights

A gold dish-shaped plaque set with green and blue sapphires (two now deficient) and decorated with 'neo-classical' shotwork, palmettes, looping ribbons and quatrefoil sections

Conclusion

Henry Murphy was such a singular and important English jeweller because of the effortless style and highly imaginative approach which he unfailingly brought to bear over a period spanning some thirty years, from neo-Gothic and Renaissance imagery through Arts and Crafts naturalism to Art Deco minimalism. His designs were stylish, original, technically superior and refreshingly innovative. As well as being an accomplished metalworker who understood the complexities of his chosen medium, he excelled in the art and application of enamel in all its forms, mastering the skills of decorative ornamentation such as repoussé, coloured golds and niello. His premature death on the eve of war in 1939 robbed the world of a truly unique goldsmith responsible for a wealth of distinctive jewellery.

Covered bowl in silver with ivory chrysoprase-topped finial and ivory and silver feet, and enriched with gold, gems and enamel, 1932

CHAPTER 3

Domestic Silver

During the first three decades of the twentieth century, domestic silver in Britain was greatly affected by radical changes in both the philosophy and the methods of design and manufacture. From the 1880s the impact of Arts and Crafts attitudes impinged increasingly upon silversmiths at every level of the market and by 1900 domestic silver was, as in many other areas of the consumer market, broadly reflecting the fashion for artistic individuality and the ideology of handcraftsmanship. On the one hand the individual silversmiths such as C.R. Ashbee, John Paul Cooper, Henry Wilson and Omar Ramsden, and the associated guilds and workshops, were promoting new styles that successfully combined the techniques of hand-craft production with historicism based on acceptably pre-industrial forms, materials and decoration. Many of these were promoted through the popular series of selling displays organised by the Arts and Crafts Exhibition Society, events that were deliberately vague in the distinctions drawn between individual and commercial production. Equally confused was the sense of style, with the wares on show reflecting medieval, Celtic, Renaissance, Tudor, Jacobean, Queen Anne and Adam forms, along with the continually influential taste for the Far East, the Islamic world, and the organic naturalism of Art Nouveau. On the other hand, commercial manufacturers, aware of this change in the nature of the marketplace and the impact of the handcraft ethic, were moving away from the emphasis on industrial methods and finishes that had dominated much of the latter part of the nineteenth century. A particularly apposite reflection of this was Liberty & Company who managed to produce ranges of silver and metalwork that were noted for their individuality

and handcraft look despite being made in quantity by commercial silversmiths in Birmingham and elsewhere.

At the same time, British designers and manufacturers generally were responding to the increased popularity of European, and notably French, styles, a taste greatly affected by the Paris

Cup or chalice with a hammered finish and Jensen-type ornaments. The date, and the present location, of this are not known, but the Scandinavian style would suggest an early date

Tazza in silver and copper, with a ring of semi-precious stones around the stem, and a chased inscription. The Arts and Crafts style of this piece and all its detailing suggest an early date, perhaps 1912-1914

Despite its early style, this tazza was made in 1931. The influence of Jensen and other Scandinavian silversmiths was, therefore, important to Murphy throughout his career

Exhibition of 1900 and the sequence of international exhibitions that followed in various European capitals, by the close trade links engendered from 1904 by the Entente Cordiale, and by the Franco-British Exhibition held in London in 1908.

Harry Murphy was a product of this period and his work, as a result, is remarkable for its stylistic diversity. No other English silversmith working through the first three decades of the twentieth century was better able to capture the full range of fashionable styles, from Renaissance

Pencil sketches of a coffee set in a classical style, and some jewellery details, early 1930s. In both shape and detail the jug and bowl are remarkably close to a coffee set made by the Swedish silversmith Jacob Angman in 1924, now in the collection of the National Museum, Stockholm

THE WORSHIPFUL COMPANY OF GOLDSMITHS

Covered porringer with niello detailing and ivory finial, 1928. This was the first piece of silver made by Murphy to be purchased by the Goldsmiths' Company for their permanent collection

THE WORSHIPFUL COMPANY OF GOLDSMITHS

Silver thermometer case, with niello decoration. This piece, in the family collection, is unmarked. Style and decoration suggest an early date, perhaps before, or shortly after, the First World War

Scaled pencil drawing for a tea and coffee set in an early 18th century style. While in many ways a committed modernist, Murphy continued throughout his career to explore historical influences, an echo of his upbringing as an Arts and Crafts silversmith

revival and Arts and Crafts to Art Deco and modernist classicism. Working initially as an apprentice and subsequently as an equal with Henry Wilson, he was inculcated with the principles of Arts and Crafts workshop practice, principles that remained with him through two decades of running a large and busy manufacturing workshop and retail outlet. However, unlike his contemporaries who worked on their own or in small like-minded groups and whose work, as a result, rarely changed or developed, Murphy, driven by the scale of his business and the need to maintain a large enterprise in the real commercial world,

Classical style five piece teaset in silver, with kingwood handles, early 1930s

was able constantly to develop his work to suit the changes in the marketplace. As a result, he was uniquely able to bring together Arts and Crafts philosophies with the needs of modern commercial design and manufacturing processes.

Throughout his career, Murphy drew upon the formative influences of his early life. From his time with Wilson he maintained both a sense of the importance of workshop practice and technical expertise along with the ability to work closely with artists and designers who offered particular skills. Also from this period came his passion for the mixing of materials and techniques, something that continued to characterise his work right up to his death.

Few records survive of the Wilson period, but there are a number of photographs of pieces apparently by Wilson that carry Murphy's name on the back. A rare survival is a design for a copper candlestick, drawn by Wilson and sent by him to Murphy from Venice in 1913, complete with detailed manufacturing instructions, including the suggestion that casts in bronze could be made

from the original in sheet metal for reasons of cheapness. A photograph of Murphy in a workshop, perhaps Kenton Street, shows a similar candlestick in the background (see page 20).

Murphy's sources were eclectic, to say the least. Among his papers preserved by the family are collections of postcards and photographs of objects in various museum collections, notably the British Museum and the Victoria & Albert. Many are of medieval enamelled metalwork, but others show medieval and later silver cups and covers and similar wares, with an emphasis on the seventeenth century. Other postcards relate more to shape design, notably three showing a nineteenth dynasty silver goat-handled vase from the Cairo Museum, a Sung dynasty Chinese porcelain vase and gold vessels from the royal graves at Ur. Echoes of all of these can be found in domestic silver designed by Murphy in the 1930s. Alongside these are floral weaving patterns of various periods, sketches of Chinese floral designs and a collection of early nineteenth century botanical watercolours, inspiration for

Tea kettle in silver, with kingwood handle, 1931

Hand raised silver presentation teaset in an Art Deco style, with ivory handle and finials, early 1930s

Hand raised three piece teaset with ivory handles, reflecting Murphy's enthusiasm for contemporary French metalwork, early 1930s

Silver and ivory teapot in a French Art Deco style, 1931

some of the floral enamel decoration of both jewellery and silver. This diversity of design sources makes Murphy a typical product of his period, a time when museum collections were maintained primarily for the purposes of design education.

Murphy's time in Germany with Lettré also had a lasting influence, even though the outcome was unhappy on a personal level. The legacy was a continuing interest in modern German design, inherent within which was the valuable experience of a European approach to Arts and

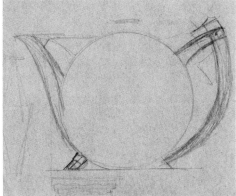

Pencil sketches for the teapot for the geometric teaset shown in Milan in 1933

Contemporary photograph of the geometric teaset in silver and kingwood, for which Murphy received a gold medal at the Milan Exhibition of 1933. Designed to be machine produced from die-stamped components, the teaset was an attempt by Murphy to make modernism available to the mass market. However, no Sheffield manufacturer took on the challenge. This set is now in the Victoria & Albert Museum, having been given in 1985 by Andrew Cox in memory of his parents

Four piece silver teaset with stylised Art Deco detailing, presented by Frank Pick as a marriage gift to Mr & Mrs Valentine, mid-1930s

This is the only other known example of the geometric teaset and was owned by Murphy's son, Brian, until his death. The coffee pot, made during the 1930s but completed after Murphy's death in 1939, was not part of the original set, as shown in Milan in 1933. Subsequently sold by Christie's, this set in now in a private collection PRIVATE TRUST

The set was well received at the time, with comments in Design for Today *and various newspapers. One journalist wrote: 'It is a striking design, and at the same time complies with practical needs. The cream jug has a lid…and the spoon on the sugar bowl fits on to a fastener and cannot be lost. The design is brilliant…but it will take a period before the general public get away from the conventional style of teaset. I do feel Mr Murphy and other designers are giving a big fillip to the silver-ware trade by such provocative and original patterns.'*

Crafts design philosophies in which industry was seen as part of the creative process rather than its antithesis. It was this experience that enabled Murphy to set up and successfully operate over a long period the Falcon Studio with its practical blend of Arts and Crafts and industrial practices, along with his ability to respond flexibly to commercial, consumer and business pressures. Murphy's subsequent visits to Germany in the 1930s were a convenient reminder of German, and European, design and manufacturing attitudes. Among the family papers are many letters and documents that underline Murphy's enthusiasm for modern German design in the fields of silver and jewellery, apart from the obvious records of attendance at exhibitions. Typical is a brochure documenting the history of the Berlin silversmith H.J.Wilm, founded in 1767. Produced in 1937, and predominantly illustrated with modern productions, this was presented to Murphy by F.R.Wilm, then the owner of what was still a family business. The scale of the Wilm workshop, the range of wares produced, the use of engraving and the blend of Arts and Crafts and modernist styles and techniques are all reminiscent of the Falcon Studio and underline the point that Murphy's whole approach was European rather than British.

Equally crucial in Murphy's development was his enthusiasm for Scandinavian metalwork in

Pencil and watercolour designs for coffee pots, mid-1930s. It is thought by some that the fashion for bomb-shaped coffee pots at this period was inspired by the Spanish Civil War

Coffee or chocolate set in silver and ivory, echoing late 17th or early 18th century models, 1935

Coffee set in silver with ivory handles, engraved with garden flowers, and with finials enriched with gold, amethysts and moonstones, mid-1930s

Coffee set in silver, with kingwood handles, classical shape with Art Deco detailing, 1931. A similar set is in the collection of the Worshipful Company of Goldsmiths

Cup and cover with niello decoration and ivory knop, early 1930s

Twelve-sided hand raised conical cup and cover, enriched with gold and enamel, ivory finial, 1930. This was given by the Goldsmiths' Company to George Ravensworth Hughes on his retirement as Clerk in 1953 PRIVATE TRUST

general, and for the work of Georg Jensen in particular. His earliest work has echoes of Jensen and this parallelism is maintained well into the 1930s. It can be seen in shapes and surface finish, in handles, stems and spouts, in finials, in various forms of applied decoration, and in the mixture of materials, notably in the use of ivory and applied gem stones. It is also important in practical terms, for clearly the workshop established by Jensen, and its method of working, was a useful model for the Falcon Studio. There are also links with other Jensen designers, for example Sigvard Bernadotte's use of fluting, and Johan Rohde's rounded shapes. This interest, supported by many documents in the family collection including a photograph of modern pieces of Scandinavian silver and pewter shown in the Imported Luxuries Exhibition held at the Goldsmiths' Hall in 1932, went beyond the work of Jensen, Michelsen and other Danish designers. References can be found to work by other Scandinavian artists, such as the Swedish silversmith,

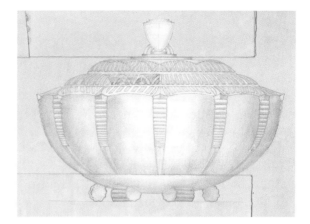

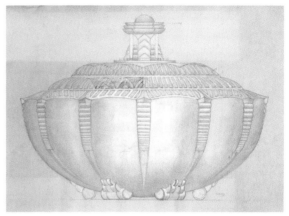

Cup and cover, stepped form, ivory and faceted lapis lazuli finial, 1939

Pencil and watercolour design for a bowl and pierced cover, with overlays offering alternative feet and finials in Art Deco style, mid-1930s. A pencilled note suggests prices: 10in., £50, 12in. £75, 15in. £100. No examples are known of this design

Jacob Angman. A teaset made by Murphy in the early 1930s is close to an Angman coffee set of 1924, in both shape and decorative detail.

A reflection of Murphy's continued interest in Scandinavia was his involvement with the Anglo-Danish Society. In 1935, to mark the Silver Jubilee of George V and Queen Mary, the Society presented the King and Queen with a pair of Royal Copenhagen vases painted with portraits of Edward VII and Queen Alexandra and views of Windsor and Fredensborg Castles. Murphy, 'the English artist in metalwork', as he

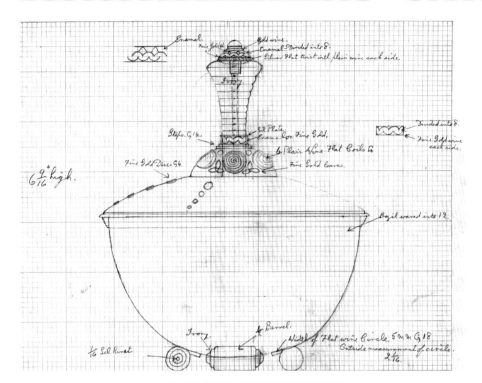

Detailed scale pencil design for a bowl and cover, enriched with gold, enamel and gems and with ivory finial and feet

Bowl and cover, made to this design in 1932   PRIVATE TRUST

Bowl and cover with coral mounted flame finial and characteristic Murphy-style Art Deco feet in cut tube, 1931. This, and other pieces in similar style, underline Murphy's continuing interest in modern German silver. Shown in the British Art in Industry Exhibition at the Royal Academy, London, in 1935
THE WORSHIPFUL COMPANY OF GOLDSMITHS

Presentation bowl and cover with niello decoration, hardstone finial and similar feet. Date unknown, probably early 1930s

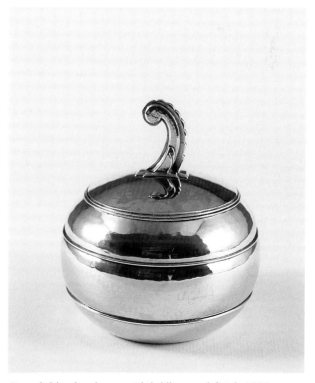

Two-handled bowl and cover with typical Murphy finial, 1934

Rounded bowl and cover with boldly curved finial, 1933

was described in the *Journal of the Anglo-Danish Society*, was commissioned to make bronze bases and covers for the vases.

Also important was his enthusiasm for modern French design, and for artist designers such as Puiforçat and Dunand. Among his papers is a photograph of lacquer-decorated vases by Dunand, a look he borrowed for a small range of silver-mounted copper bowls and vases made at the Falcon Studio. A reflection of his continuing attachment to France was his significant contribution to the Paris Exhibition of 1937 and his visit to it with a group of British designers and silversmiths.

As a designer and silversmith working in the commercial arena, Murphy had also to be constantly aware of what was going on in his own field. He collected photographs of modern

Cigarette canister with engraved abstract foliate decoration and poppy finial, 1938. This was made to be shown at the International Exhibition of Handicrafts in Berlin in 1938, Murphy being a prime mover of British participation
THE WORSHIPFUL COMPANY OF GOLDSMITHS

Three examples of one of the most characteristic productions of Murphy and the Falcon Studio, the rosebowl with pierced cover. A number of these are known, following the same basic form but with many variations in the details, notably the base, the stem and the finial. There are examples in the collections of the Victoria & Albert Museum, the Royal Academy and the Worshipful Company of Goldsmiths. The style of the piercing also varies, but most follow the principle of tree of life panels. Left: Pierced base and stem and silver finial, 1935; opposite above: solid base and ivory and opal finial, 1939; opposite below: pierced shield base, finial enriched with enamel and gems, 1939

Another favourite Murphy form, the circular cigarette box with tight-fitting cover. Again, many of these are known, with many variations in design and details. This example, known only from a photograph, features the 'traffic-light' gem-set finial. A note on the back of the photograph gives the price, £8.8s.0d. (£8.40p). This box was presented to the Royal Academy of Arts in 1933 by the painter Algernon Talmage, RA

Cigarette box with raised Art Deco-style decoration and engraved curved motifs that echo the finial and explore in a playful manner the theme of smoking, 1933. Shown in the British Art in Industry Exhibition at the Royal Academy, London, in 1935

THE WORSHIPFUL COMPANY OF GOLDSMITHS

Three cigarette boxes with formal geometric or architectural decoration and ivory and gem-set finials. Left to right: 1934, 1930, 1932

Cigarette box with applied wire roundels and a turned ivory finial, 1931. A pioneering example of abstract modernism, underlining how closely Murphy was in touch with contemporary Art Deco styles. Shown in the British Art in Industry Exhibition at the Royal Academy, London, in 1935

Trinket box with domed cover and gem-set finial, decorated with engraved hunting scenes. The designer and engraver was Ethel Auger, a student at the Central School of Arts and Crafts. The original version, with elaborate castle finial, was made in 1927 and is in the collection of the Worshipful Company of Goldsmiths. This version, made in 1929 and also engraved by Auger, has full Murphy and Falcon Studio marks

work by rivals, a series of which he used to illustrate talks on modern silver. Among these are groups of domestic wares by Elkington, Wakeley & Wheeler, Roberts & Belk, Adie Brothers, Mappin & Webb, Omar Ramsden, Comyns and Claridge's. In most cases these show work in a commercial Art Deco style, with echoes of European modernism not marked by particular originality. Clearly, when giving talks, Murphy used to pass comments on the work of his commercial rivals, and some of these survive. For example, a fruit dish designed by Harold Stabler for Wakeley & Wheeler is described as 'a piece with definite character and individuality'. Two circular boxes mounted with jade and coral by Cartier, not too dissimilar to Murphy's own work, are called 'charming and interesting'. On

the other hand, he is dismissive of Claridge's new plate: 'Designed by a lady architect, and as architects can do no wrong, I will not express an opinion on this…It is a misconception to suppose no one capable of designing new flat ware unless an architect…'. Despite these views, he was friends with a number of architects, notably Sir Edwin Lutyens and Edward Maufe.

Murphy was a regular lecturer and a practised teacher through his association with the Central School of Arts and Crafts. It is not surprising, therefore, that he had strong views about the state of art and design in general, and the silver and jewellery trade in particular, that he frequently expressed. Some of these lectures survive, including one given to a formal gathering in the 1930s. This reveals many of his ideas, namely that

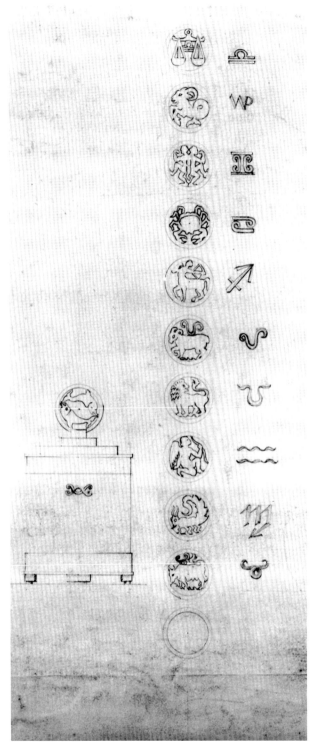

Pencil drawing showing a version of the cigarette box with signs of the zodiac finials, based on the series of pierced silver zodiac brooches (see page 67). No examples are known

Wooden cigarette box mounted with silver disc engraved with Eric Gill-style athletic figures, 1934. It is likely this was made by Murphy for his own use

Paul de Lamerie was the 'starting point of modern design', that Morris had little effect on the commercial silversmith and so the work of Wilson, Ashbee and Ramsden was 'known to a very limited circle, and to the trade, not at all', and that design was stifled by reproduction and period work: 'we are overwhelmed with period furniture, period houses, singly and in rows, disfigure the countryside, period silversmiths' work gluts the shops'. He also expresses his enthusiasm for Europe: 'Contemporary design has made little or no impression on the English manufacturer, while on the Continent much of the silver has responded to the modern feeling, notably in France, Sweden and Denmark'. Later, he continues on the same theme: 'European craftsmen have for the past 20 years been creating new and fresh forms in silver. Among these craftsmen are artists who have caught the real spirit of modernism…these men are moved by an aesthetic philosophy close to the spirit of the times which insists on results obtained by vigorous attention to functional requirements,

Maser-style wooden bowl with silver base and mounts, engraved with motto Preserve For Our Use The Kindly Fruits Of The Earth, 1931 PRIVATE TRUST

Large fluted oval fruit bowl, 1938. This bowl, hand raised by Murphy and S. Hammond, is a masterpiece of technical silversmithing. Hammond was teaching with Murphy at the Central School of Arts and Crafts THE WORSHIPFUL COMPANY OF GOLDSMITHS

and the simple straight-forward use of materials'.

However, as befits one of the first generation of Royal Designers for Industry, Murphy's primary concern was for training and apprenticeship schemes, and workshop practices that maintained the traditional skills of his industry while encouraging the process of design from within the trade. As one of the generation brought up to believe in the marriage of art and industry, he understood the benefits of machine production and modern technology as something that challenged rather than threatened the designer and artist. At the same time, he had little patience with the contemporary fashion for involving outsiders in the design process: 'The occasional incursions of outside designers, sculptors and architects, and even of unattached artist-craftsmen, have rarely proved stimulating to the trade; on the contrary, they have sometimes excited justifiable adverse criticism'. Particularly relevant, in the context of the time, is his reference to the 'unattached artist-craftsmen'.

Tall fluted vase, in a classic Art Deco style, from a set of six designed by Murphy and Professor R.Y. Gleadowe in 1936 for use of the Livery tables of the Goldsmiths' Company. In 1938 a replica was made, commissioned by the Goldsmiths' Company as a gift for Sir Crisp English to commemorate the inception of the Warden's Silver Committee during his year of office as Prime Warden, 1937-38 THE WORSHIPFUL COMPANY OF GOLDSMITHS

Large oval fruit bowl, engraved with Art Nouveau style foliate decoration, 1936

Tall, plain trumpet-shaped vase, 1935

Tall onion-shaped vase on tall base and bowl and cover with curved finial, dates unknown, probably mid-1930s. A very similar finial is on the bowl and cover shown on page 89

Small beaker and bowl, with niello decoration, 1932

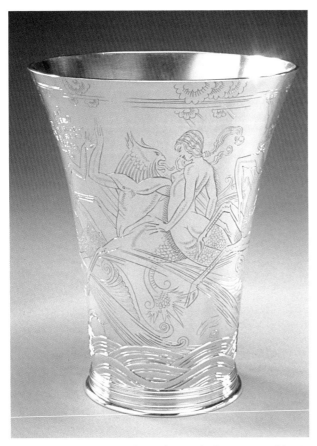

The Sea Beaker, designed by Professor Gleadowe, engraved by G. Friend with a frieze of mermaids and sea creatures and made by Murphy, 1929. This is an early example of cooperative craftsmanship between the three friends. Shown at the Exhibition of Modern Silverwork at Goldsmiths' Hall, 1938

Flared commemorative beaker, made for Isabella Dione Mitchell, perhaps a relative of Murphy's one-time business partner, J.P. Mitchell, and engraved, possibly by Friend, with a classical female figure floating above waves, date unknown, probably mid-1930s

Loving cup supported by stylised horse handles rising from a flat base, engraved with a lively classical frieze of female figures and horses, perhaps by Friend, date unknown, probably early 1930s

Two tankards, one of a faceted flared form with a Jensen-like handle, the other trumpet shape with flared base and scroll handle on Art Deco leaf mounts, dates unknown, 1930s

Tankard, traditional 17th century form, 1936

Tankard, traditional 17th century form with chased inscription below the rim, date unknown, possibly late 1920s

interested in designing for the jewellery and silversmithing trade should identify themselves with the trade, understand its problems, work within its limitations as well as its possibilities, and accept its remuneration'.

It was these and other concerns that compelled Murphy to bring together in his own work design and manufacturing skills and to maintain, at considerable financial and emotional cost, a silversmith's workshop of the kind that would have been familiar to a specialised craftsman working two centuries earlier. Such workshops, which genuinely combined art and industry, were by then almost unknown in Britain, while

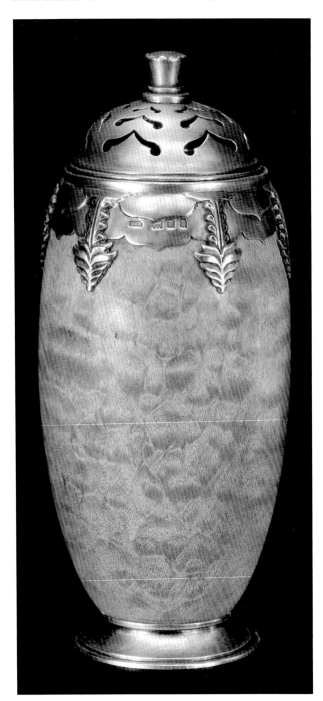

Turned wood sugar dredger with silver mounts, 1930

Dredger with engraved foliate decoration and ball pyramid finial, 1937

The lecture makes it clear he is thinking of people like Wilson who '…have not had the influence they deserve, partly because the trade was not able to benefit from their genius, but also because they were remote and worked in circumstances which were not those of the trade. To be in an industry but not of it diminishes both usefulness and influence. People who are really

Family of condiments, and a dredger, various dates, early 1930s. The dredger, shown in the British Art in Industry Exhibition at the Royal Academy, London, 1935, is in the collection of the Worshipful Company of Silversmiths

Pepper pot and two salts, 1937 and 1938

Publicity photograph showing eggcup and spoon, and set of condiments (mustard, pepper, salt), date unknown, probably early 1930s. The hand-written caption notes that the plate was by A.E. Gray & Company, a Staffordshire pottery famous for launching the career of Susie Cooper

Set of eggcups in the matted finish favoured by Murphy for a while in the 1930s, a style reflecting contemporary German inspiration, date unknown

Doughnut-shaped eggcup, 1932

Container for Tiptree jam with attached spoon, both featuring the typical Murphy ball pyramid finial, a style echoing Jensen, date unknown, mid-1930s

Tea strainer with gold bead decoration and typical pierced handle, 1935

still common in Europe. At the same time, his insistence on a direct relationship both with the trade, through his professional position, and with the buying public, through his retail outlet, enabled him to avoid those issues of remoteness and self-satisfied superiority that seemed inherent in the Arts and Crafts Movement in Britain.

The range and diversity of domestic silver produced by Murphy and the Falcon Studio was, as a result, quite remarkable. Early pieces, produced before the First World War and in the early 1920s, are hard to identify with certainty. A group of tazzas, dishes and a chalice, all now lost, have all the style characteristics of this period and

Set of four caddy spoons, with pierced tree of life handles, exhibiting subtle differences, various dates from 1929

Low-sided bowl, possibly wine taster, with ivory handle, 1935

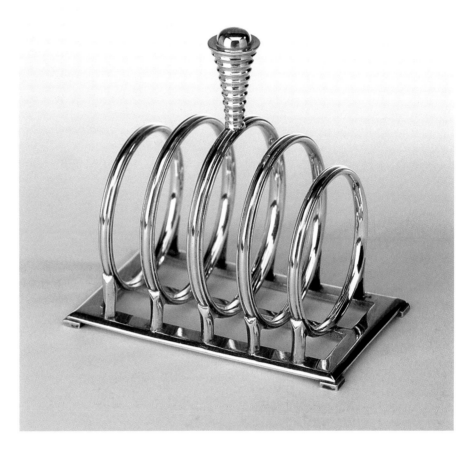

Ring-form toastrack, 1938

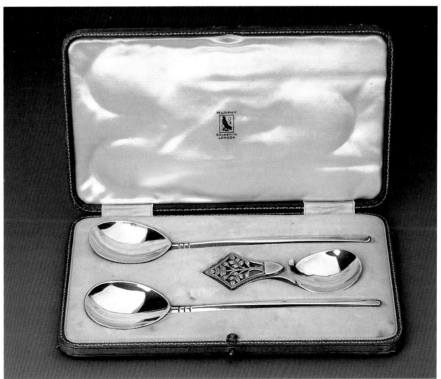

Set of caddy and serving spoons, in original green leather Falcon Studio box, 1937-38

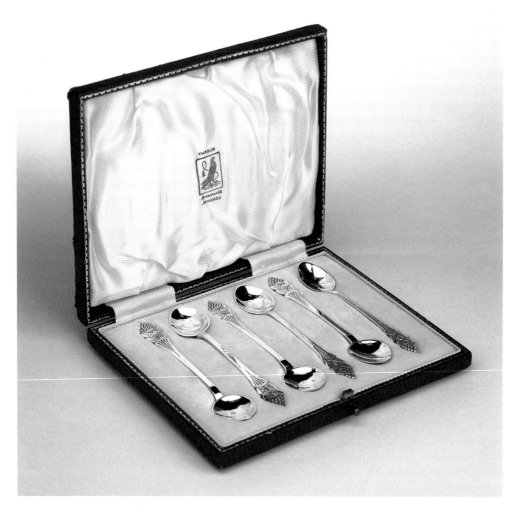

Set of teaspoons in original Falcon Studio box, 1933

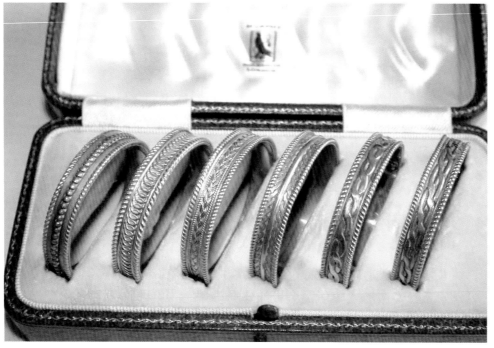

Set of napkin rings with chased decoration in original Falcon Studio box, 1930s

Set of spoons mounted with cabochon gemstones, faceted stone 1929, all others 1931

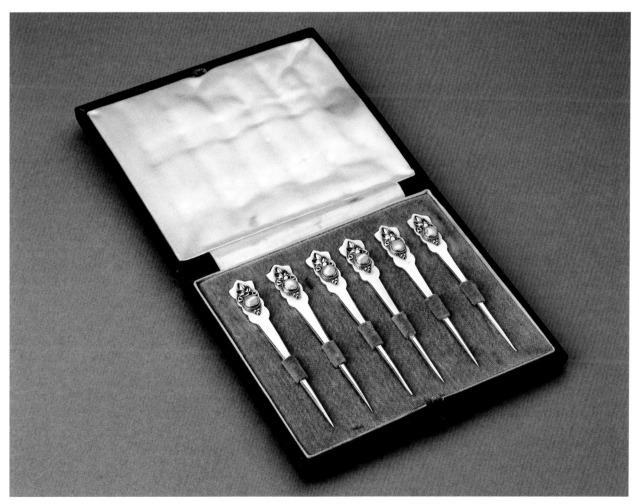

Set of pearl-mounted cocktail sticks in original Falcon Studio box, 1930

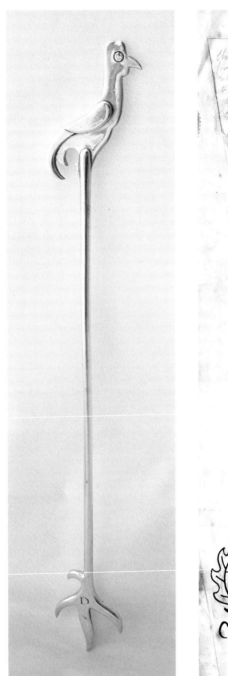

Cock cocktail stick, 1935

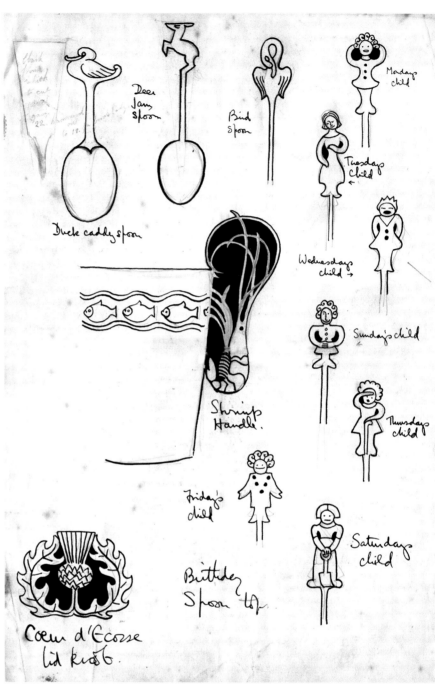

Pencil and ink drawing showing the designs for the figure tops for the series of days of the week children's spoons, along with other animal and bird spoons, a shrimp bowl handle and a thistle knop

show, at the same time, a strong dependence on Jensen and other Scandinavian designers. However, such pieces were still being made in the mid-1930s and so style cannot be relied upon as a means of dating. Also early are decorative items such as a thermometer stand decorated with niello engraving and cabochon gems.

Murphy's enthusiasm for niello, which he developed during his time with Wilson, seems to be characteristic of early, pre-Falcon Studio pieces. Apart from dating difficulties, the problem raised by pieces before 1928 is the uncertainty of where they were actually made. Likely locations seem to be the workshops at the Central School

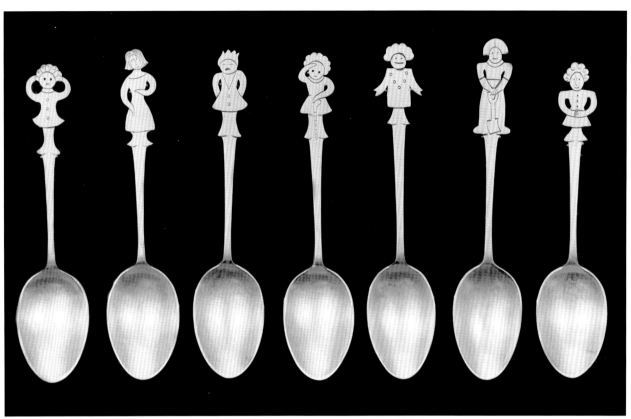

Full set of the days of the week children's spoons, hand made in quantity during the latter part of the 1930s. 'Monday's child is fair of face, Tuesday's child is full of grace, Wednesday's child is full of woe, Thursday's child has far to go, Friday's child is loving and giving, Saturday's child works hard for a living. The child who is born on the Sabbath day is bonny and bright and good and gay'

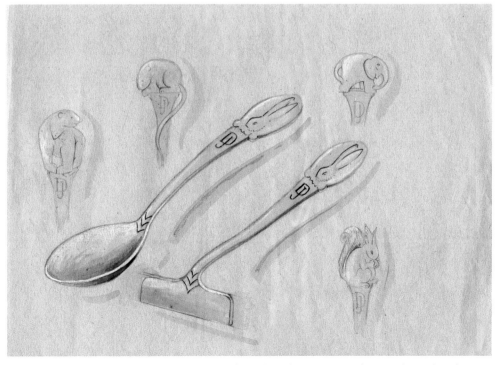

Watercolour design for a spoon and pusher set, to be made with various animal tops and initials, to be given as Christening presents

Service of cutlery in a contemporary Scandinavian style, made in 1933-4

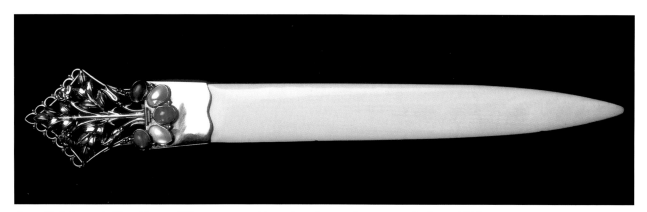

Ivory-bladed paperknife, gold tree of life mount set with pearls and green chrysoprase cabochons, 1930s

of Arts and Crafts or Wilson's studio in Kent. However, the main production period, from the workshops in Weymouth Street and Marylebone High Street, was between 1928 and 1939, and most pieces known today date from this time.

The output of domestic silver from the Falcon Studio included tea and coffee wares, jugs, bowls, vases, tazzas and covered cups, tankards and mugs, ranges of cutlery, cruets, condiments, salts and sugar sifters, toast racks, napkin rings, Christening

Five-branch candelabrum made for Baron Manners, date unknown, probably late 1930s

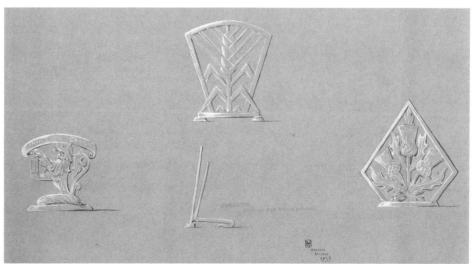

Watercolour design for menu holders, with fitting detail, dated 1935. No examples are known

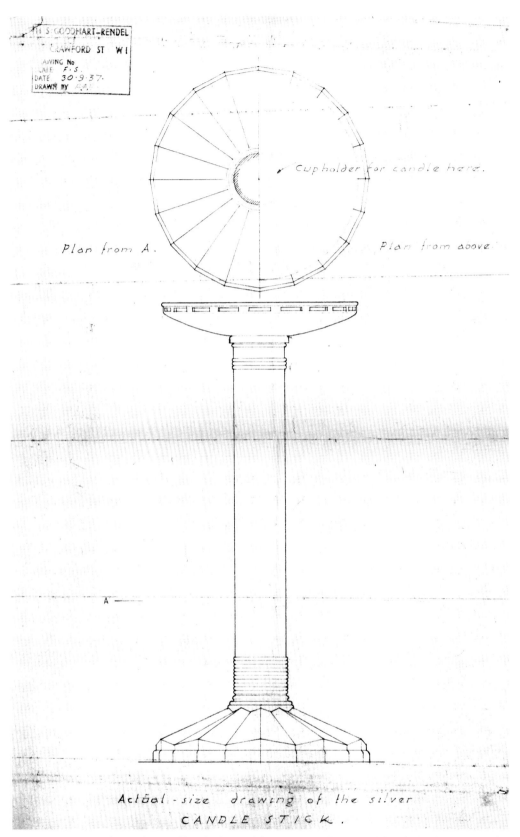

Text within the drawing:

H S GOODHART-RENDEL
CRAWFORD ST W1
AWING No
DATE F.S.
DATE 30.9.37.
DRAWN BY

Cup holder for candle here.

Plan from A.   Plan from above.

A

Actual-size drawing of the silver
CANDLE STICK.

Architect's drawing for a silver candlestick, designed by H.S. Goodhart-Rendel and dated 30 September 1937. Goodhart-Rendel, a well-known modernist architect responsible for, among other buildings, the Hay's Wharf offices by London Bridge, now regarded as one of London's best Art Deco buildings, often worked with artists and designers outside the architectural profession

Louis Galvin completed his apprenticeship to Murphy in 1935 and marked the event by making, under Murphy's supervision, a set of four candlesticks, one of which he is holding here

Pair of candlesticks by Murphy from the Goodhart-Rendel design, made in memory of Robert Bruxner, 1938

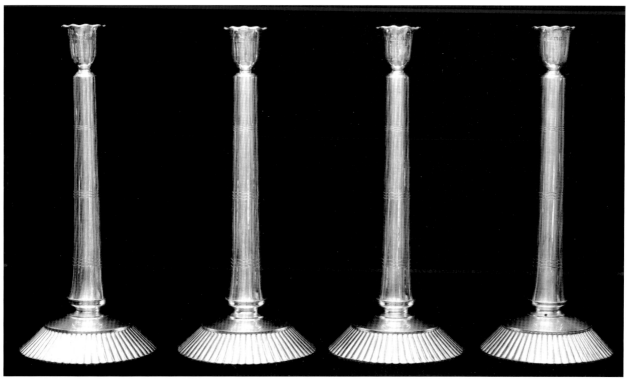

The set of candlesticks made by Galvin in 1935-36. These were originally commissioned by a client in Essex, but remained at the Falcon Studio and were purchased by Galvin from Murphy's widow after his death in 1939. Subsequently they were split into two pairs, one of which was bought by the Victoria & Albert Museum in 1973

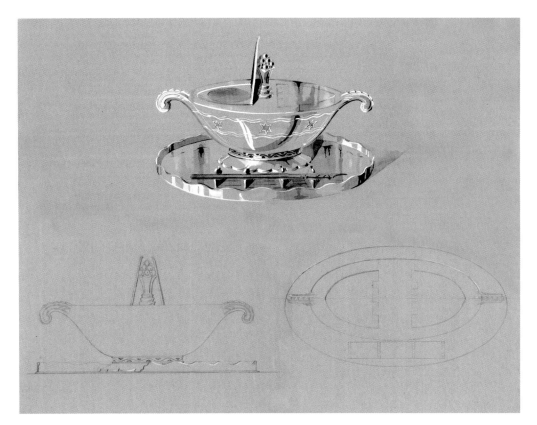

Pencil and watercolour design for a desk inkstand, in a classical style with Art Deco details, including the familiar ball pyramid finial, mid-1930s. Various inkstand designs by Murphy exist, but no matching examples are known

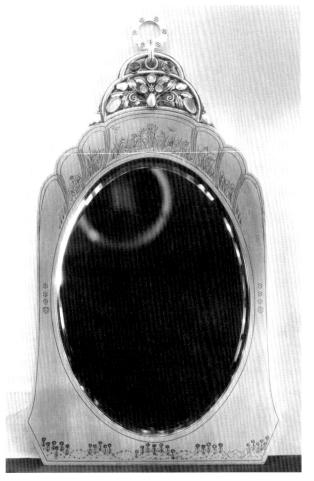

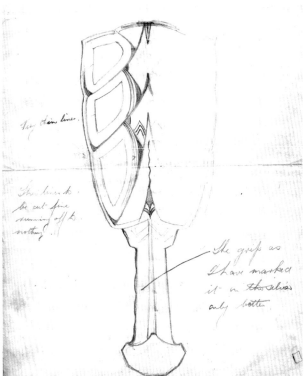

Pencil design for a dressing table hand mirror in silver and niello

Frame for a hanging mirror, decorated with niello flowers and set with gemstones. Date and present location unknown, but the Arts and Crafts style suggests an early date, perhaps in the 1920s

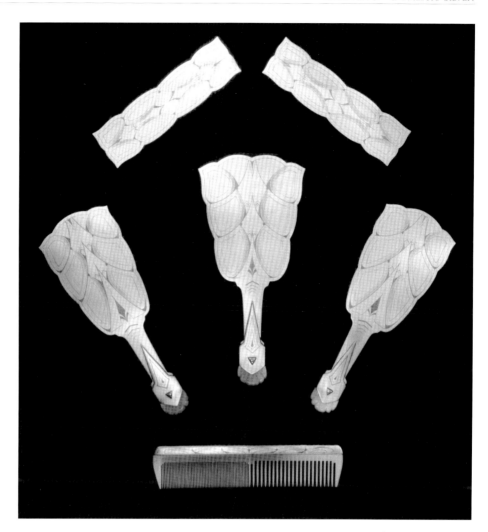

Dressing table set comprising hand mirror, brushes and comb, with niello decoration, date unknown, but probably early 1930s. This set was bought by a client in Victoria, British Columbia

Boxed set of dressing table brushes with floral engraving and ivory-finished handles, 1935

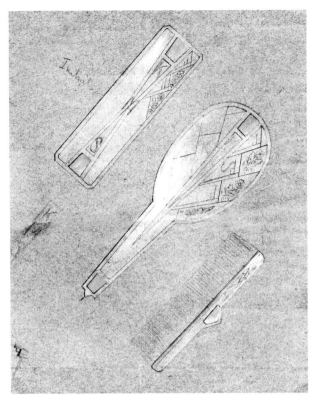

Pencil and watercolour design for a dressing table set in silver, enamel and niello

Dressing table hand mirror mounted with a high quality needlepoint garden scene in a typically 1920s style, 1938

Dressing table set comprising mirror, brushes and comb, with chased and engraved decoration, 1933

116

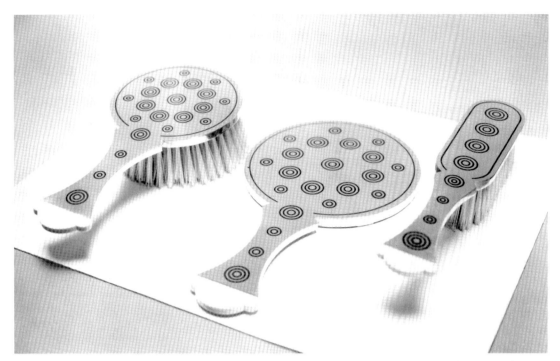

Part dressing table set comprising mirror and two brushes, with niello decoration in concentric circles, 1934. Shown in the British Art in Industry Exhibition at the Royal Academy, London, in 1935

THE WORSHIPFUL COMPANY OF GOLDSMITHS

sets and children's wares, mirrors and dressing table sets, strainers and sauceboats, candlesticks and candelabra, cigarette boxes and other covered boxes and bowls and inkstands, along with many other domestic and decorative items. There are oddities such as ceremonial trowels and an auctioneer's gavel, everything indicative of large scale workshop production aimed primarily at the retail trade. The surviving order and production record books underline that this diversity was driven as much by commercial necessity as by creativity.

Although stylistically diverse, these pieces all carry the Murphy hallmark, in both a literal and a generic way. There are many reflections of eighteenth century forms and styles, but these are never used in a conventional revivalist way. Each one carries at the same time the clear stamp of its period. The best traditions of the Arts and Crafts Movement are often present, in the quality of conception, in the individuality of design, in the controlled use of ornament and the mixing of materials, and in the sheer skill of manufacture. However, as before, these elements are free of the heavy hand of historicism and belong clearly to

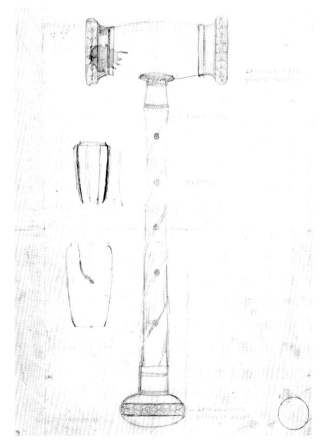

Pencil design for an auctioneer's gavel, with chased laurel leaf bands, date unknown

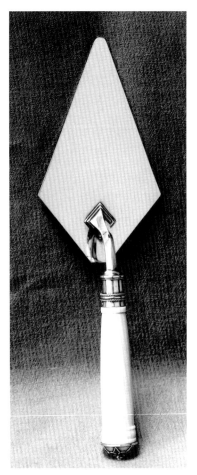

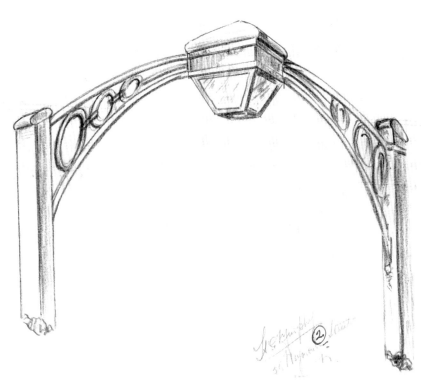

Pencil sketch for a lamp and supporting arch in metalwork, perhaps bronze, one of a number of surviving designs for large scale or architectural work by Murphy

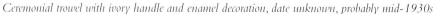

Ceremonial trowel with ivory handle and enamel decoration, date unknown, probably mid-1930s

A pair of Royal Copenhagen vases, depicting Queen Alexandra and King Edward VII, with images of Fredensborg and Windsor Castles on the verso, presented by the Anglo-Danish Society to King George V and Queen Mary to celebrate their Silver Jubilee in 1935. The bronze bases and ornamental covers were made by Murphy

Bronze mount for a globe, featuring the signs of the zodiac, possibly made by Murphy for his family. Present location and date unknown. Visible on the side table are a pair of the bird and animal bookends in brass and enamel, a hammered silver vase and the wooden cigarette box with silver disc on the lid, illustrated on page 94

First World War memorial plaque, designed by Murphy for St Mary's Platt, Kent

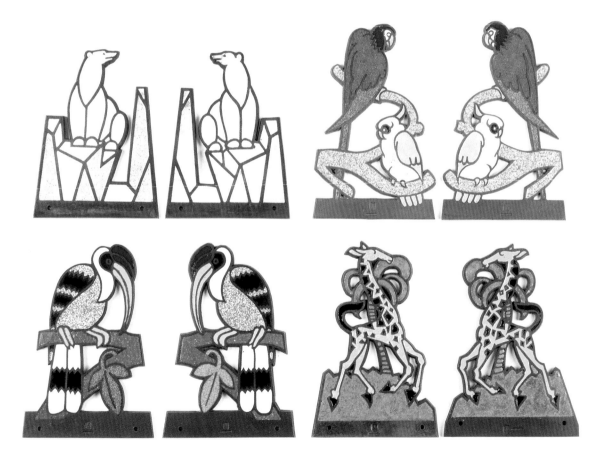

Pairs of animal and bird plaques for bookends, made in enamel and brass. Entertaining, colourful and dynamic, these represented an attempt by Murphy to broaden the production of the Falcon Studio into a more popular market, and thus relieve some of the perennial financial problems. Success was probably limited, as most of the surviving sets were still at the studio after Murphy's death

Pair of penguin bookends in enamel on brass, mounted on wood, 1930s. These may be the pair on the side table on page 119

Louis Galvin at work preparing or painting enamels, with some of the bookends on the table, mid-1930s

Design for the lemur bookends, and the finished pair, ready for mounting on to wood. They carry Falcon Studio stamps

the modern world. At the same time, many pieces show a flawless comprehension of modernity and Art Deco styling while avoiding the banal and the excessive, elements that affected so much domestic design of this period. This modernity can be seen in shape, in decoration and detail, in elements like handles, bases and knops and in the broad understanding of the contemporary fashion for timeless functionalism. As a result, there are many echoes, not just of modern European silver but also of other equivalent areas of design and manufacture, such as the pottery designed for Wedgwood by the architect Keith Murray. This approach was also reflected by Murphy's regular cooperation with specialist designers and craftsmen, such as the engravers Gooden and Friend, whose linear style has echoes of Eric Gill and other contemporary artists, the sculptor Richard Garbe and the designer Professor Gleadowe.

Domestic silver by Murphy and the Falcon Studio has a distinct look and a particular quality that makes it outstanding in its period. Among

the huge range of production are classic pieces, clearly Murphy favourites, for example the rose bowls with their pierced covers, the gem-set and ivory-mounted circular cigarette boxes and the mugs, beakers, tankards and vases enlivened with friezes of Eric Gill-like engravings. Certain design details are characteristic of Murphy, for example his fascination with knops and his regular use of pierced panels representing the tree of life. Equally distinct is his confident handling of modernism, in his shapes, in his detail and decoration and in his willingness to explore concepts such as functionalism, abstract geometry and the applications of machine manufacture, elements that go far beyond the conventional language of Art Deco design and decoration. There are, as a result, wares that reflect an extreme modernism, for example cutlery whose shape seems more of the 1960s than the 1930s and the famous circular teaset with its triangular-set kingwood handles, well known through a classic Victoria & Albert Museum poster of the

1990s (see page 10). This set, part of Murphy's gold medal-winning display at the Milan exhibition of 1933 and illustrated at the time in magazines such as *The Studio,* was a conscious attempt by Murphy to come to terms with the age of the machine. He designed the set to be mass-produced in large quantities by a mechanical die-stamping process so that the proposed retail price would be around £20. His aim, to make high quality modern design available to a wide market at an accessible price, was thwarted as no manufacturer was prepared to take up the idea.

Many designs survive, from rough sketches to finished workshop drawings. These reveal the fertility of Murphy's imagination and his skills as a draughtsman, skills shared by those in his employment. Drawings were also used to demonstrate ideas to clients and to direct the craftsmen in the workshop. At the same time a 'back of the envelope' designer and an accomplished artist, Murphy used his drawing skills to explore, to experiment, to sell and to direct. His skills as a designer, draughtsman, maker, manager and salesman enabled the Falcon Studio to survive through a long period of economic uncertainty and commercial unpredictability. In the process of this continual struggle, Murphy established himself as Britain's leading independent jeweller and silversmith, a position reflected by his professional standing: Freeman of the City of London, Liveryman of the Goldsmiths' Company, Royal Designer for Industry and Master of the RDI Faculty at the Royal College of Art, Principal of the Central School of Arts and Crafts, President of the Arts and Crafts Exhibition Society. He also sat on various committees associated with craft, design and education and was a regular visitor to trade shows in Britain and Europe in an official capacity. Given more time, he would also have accepted the offer to become Master of the Art Workers' Guild.

Bowl and covered vase in hand raised copper, the vase with applied silver decoration in a style reminiscent of French Art Deco lacquerwork. These pieces, which carry Falcon Studio stamps, indicate Murphy's desire to broaden the range of wares being made at the Falcon Studio and to cater for the cheaper market in the later 1930s

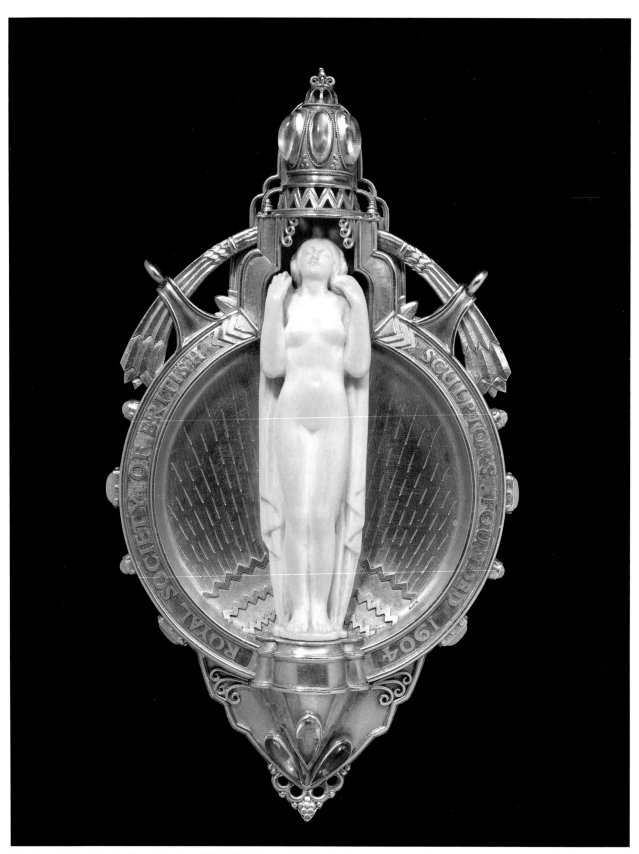

President's badge for the Royal Society of British Sculptors, 1932. This badge, incorporating a figure in ivory by Richard Garbe, and from a design by Garbe, Professor of Sculpture at the Royal College of Art and a friend of Murphy, is a glorious creation in gold, enamel and gems. The chain incorporates the names of previous presidents of the Society

CHAPTER 4

Civic and Corporate Work

A major source of employment for the Falcon Studio during the interwar period was the production of pieces commissioned by civic, corporate and institutional clients. Indeed, the speed with which the Studio was established from its foundation in 1928 owes much to this kind of work. Ranging in style from the adventurous to the pedestrian, these items, often elaborate in both conception and construction, represented in many cases more the taste of the commissioning body than the maker. Some were designed and made wholly by Murphy while others reflected a partnership with other designers, a way of working that was commonplace in the Falcon Studio. In many ways, it was Murphy's willingness to cooperate with other designers, artists and specialists such as engravers that set him apart from his contemporaries. This habit, probably developed at the start of his career in the Wilson workshop, not only ensured employment for his workforce but also greatly increased the diversity of his output. Murphy probably worked on such pieces when he was with Wilson, and at least one, a chalice-shaped cup with two lion-mounted handles made for a City of London institution, dates from 1913, the Kenton Street era.

The diversity is also underlined by the range of Murphy's clients, which included councils and local authorities, City of London livery companies, trades federations, institutions such as the Royal Institute of British Architects, the Royal Society of Arts, the Royal Academy and the Port of London Authority, the Freemasons and corporations and businesses, such as the Orient Line. There was also a steady output of work commissioned by private clients, to mark both business and family events.

By its nature, much of this commissioned work was complex, involving all aspects of silversmithing including engraving and niello work, along with an extensive use of enamelling and jewelling. Many of the pieces have, therefore, a splendour in appearance and ornamentation that, again, reflects Murphy's training under Wilson. Notable in this category is a series of chairmen's or presidents' badges of office, splendid and richly decorated gems whose modelled details and colourful enamels are

The earliest known example of Murphy's corporate work, the City of London cup of 1913

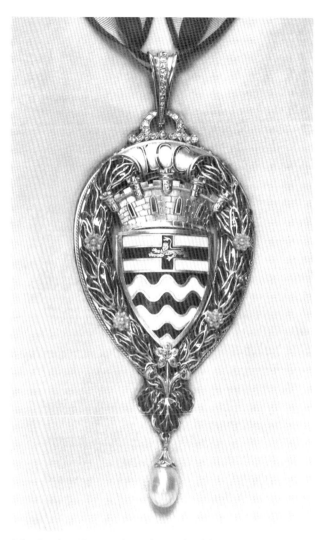

The watercolour design and the completed badge for the Chairman of the London County Council, completed by Murphy in 1927, before the setting up of the Falcon Studio. The badge survives, but in an altered state, having been crudely adapted to suit the initials of the Greater London Council

Sir George Hume, chairman of the London County Council, wearing the badge after the presentation ceremony at County Hall on 27 February 1927. At the time it was described as: 'a handsome affair, designed in collaboration with Mr. F.V.Burridge, Principal of the Central School of Arts and Crafts, by that clever young craftsman, Mr.H.G.Murphy.'

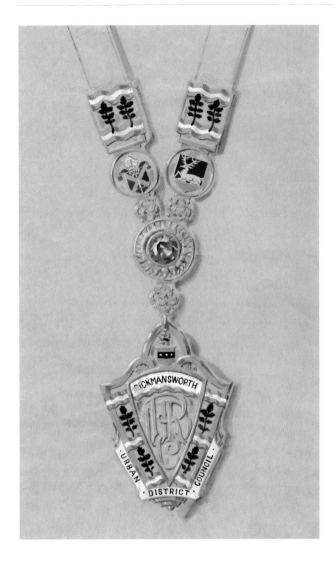

President or Chairman's badge for The Ancient Society of College Youths, made in 1937 to celebrate that institution's tercentenary

Watercolour design for the Chairman's badge for Rickmansworth Urban District Council, early 1930s

reminders both of Murphy's lasting fascination with the Renaissance and his early training in the atmosphere of the Arts and Crafts Movement. Among the more impressive of these are the badge made in 1927 for the London County Council, a glorious but traditional confection of enamel, pearls and diamonds and, in a more contemporary style, that made for Rickmansworth Urban District Council. The LCC badge is one of the earliest, predating the establishment of the Falcon Studio. The badge made for the Golders Green Parliament in 1928 is a simpler version of the LCC one, while of the same date is the badge for the West Essex Chapter of the Essex, Cambridge & Hertfordshire Society of Architects, a complex design in silver, gold, niello and cloisonné enamel. Far more traditional

in its form and modelling is the badge made in 1937 to mark the tercentenary of the Ancient Society of College Youths, a piece with an almost Victorian quality. Others include a striking badge for the British Society of Radiology while a pair of surviving watercolours show related designs of 1930 for the badges for the Metropolitan Branch of the BMA and the BDA, indications of the amount of work involved in commissions of this kind with their inevitably complicated style and budget conditions. The most complex, and in many ways the least typical, is that made for the Chairman of the Northern Builders Employers' Federation, with its Wilson-style chain inset with enamel badges representing bricklayers, carpenters, glaziers, painters, masons, plumbers,

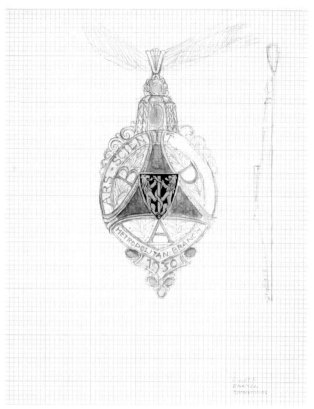

Watercolour sketch for the Chairman's badge for the Metropolitan Branch of the BDA

President or Chairman's badge for the British Society of Radiology

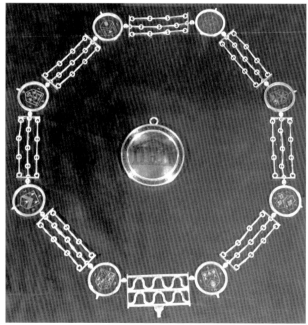

Chairman's badge and chain for the Northern Builders Employers' Federation, early 1930s

joiners and plasterers. Made primarily in gold, this was designed by M. Walker, with the Falcon Studio as manufacturer. However, the most exciting by far is the badge made for the president of the Royal Society of British Sculptors, a splendidly rich roundel in gold, enamel and jewels that is the mount for an ivory sculpture of a nude by Richard Garbe.

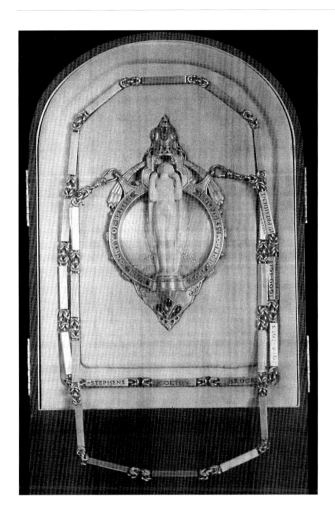

President's badge for the Royal Society of British Sculptors, with chain and box

Preliminary watercolour sketch for the chairman's badge for the West Essex Chapter of the Essex, Camb & Herts Society of Architects

Falcon Studio presentation design for an armorial badge, with oak tree motif, silver, 1933

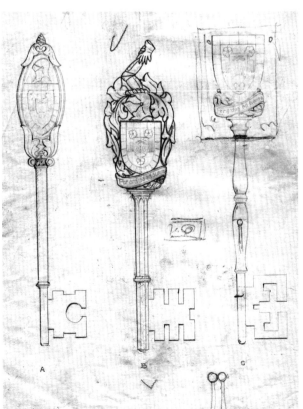

Top left: Ceremonial key for Wallington Fire Brigade, Surrey

Left: Pencil designs for ceremonial keys, early 1930s

Top right: Masonic badge for Panmure Lodge, No 715. Murphy was a member of this Lodge and produced a number of fairly conventional Masonic pieces

Bottom right: Gold and enamel lapel pin, with Persian Royal Insignia, 1930s

Enamel armorial plaque, found in the Falcon Studio after Murphy's death, a version of the plaque that forms the centre of the alms dish made for the Worshipful Company of Weaver. See page 133

Closely related, and in some ways a Murphy speciality, are the ceremonial keys in silver and enamel made for a variety of institutions such as Lincoln Butter Market and Wallington Fire Brigade. The variety of modelled decoration surrounding the enamel badges reveals Murphy's inventiveness when faced with the challenge of a predictable and repetitive form. A Freemason himself, Murphy also designed a number of more conventional masonic pieces, notably for his own Panmure Lodge.

Livery companies were important clients, a reflection of Murphy's standing during the 1930s, and the range of work is, as a result, extensive. Exacting in their demands, and

inevitably driven by a traditional approach to style and design, livery companies represented a challenge that clearly Murphy enjoyed, thanks in part to his ability to work in a variety of styles. The Weavers' Company commissioned a number of items, remarkable in their diversity. Most splendid is the mace, a notably successful blend by Murphy of a traditional form and a modern style of decoration. Strongly Art Deco in its detail, the mace was clearly a complicated design challenge, as indicated by the number of sketches and working drawings that survive, all significantly different in detail. More overtly modern is the alms dish, with its stylised Art Deco enamel centre and border details. By

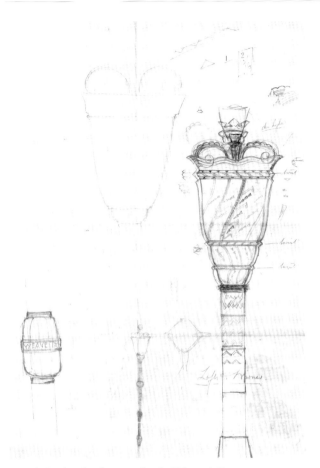

Pencil sketches for the mace for the Weavers' Company

comparison the pair of three-branch candlesticks of 1935 are surprisingly conventional, a reflection no doubt of the taste of the commissioner. Even more traditional are the salts made for Lincoln's Inn. A successful blend of old and new is represented by the coffee pots made for the Merchant Taylors' Company, an exciting combination of silver and ivory that marries together the styles of the early eighteenth century and the 1920s. A more traditional set in a mid-eighteenth century style relieved by Art Deco detailing was made for the Goldsmiths' Company. Other examples are the alms dish made in 1936 for the Carpenters' Company, a simple piece with typical Murphy foliate piercing, and the dish presented by Harry Catt to the Company of Watermen and Lightermen. Made right at the end of Murphy's life, this has

Livery silver for the Worshipful Company of Weavers: the mace (opposite), a pair of candelabra 18in. high, made in 1935 and an alms dish, notable for the enamel plaque at the centre and the Art Deco detailing of the rim. Shown in the Exhibition of Modern Silverwork at Goldsmiths' Hall, 1938

Pair of silvergilt salts for Lincoln's Inn

Coffee pots in silver and ivory for the Worshipful Company of Merchant Taylors. Shown in the Exhibition of Modern Silverwork at Goldsmiths' Hall, 1938

Alms dish presented to the Worshipful Company of Carpenters on 10 March 1936, to commemorate the centenary of the birth of Benjamin Jacob, Master in 1892, by his sons and grandsons, also members of the Company. Shown in the Exhibition of Modern Silverwork at Goldsmiths' Hall, 1938

an elegant simplicity enlivened by repeating enamel flower panels and a finely engraved calligraphic inscription.

When freed from the conventions of civic and livery company approaches to style, Murphy was able to be more adventurous. His work for the Royal Institute of British Architects reveals his true colours as a dedicated modernist who, none the less, never disregarded the importance of his Arts and Crafts background. Most remarkable are

the table centres made for the RIBA Dinner Club, a combination of glass, silver and ivory that shows Murphy's constant awareness of European, and particularly French, Art Deco design. The Arts and Crafts element is represented by the applied RIBA badges. More obvious in its Arts and Crafts background is the rose bowl and cover presented to the RIBA Dinner Club in 1937 by P.E. Thomas, the RIBA's President from 1935 to 1937. This is a favourite Murphy form, of which

Alms dish presented by Harry Jacob Catt to the Worshipful Company of Watermen and Lightermen in 1939, one of the last pieces made by Murphy at the Falcon Studio

Table centre in silver, glass and ivory, made for the Dinner Club of the Royal Institute of British Architects

Rose bowl and cover, commissioned in 1937 by P.E. Thomas, President of the Royal Institute of British Architects from 1933 to 1937, and presented by him to the RIBA Dinner Club. Shown in the Exhibition of Modern Silverwork at Goldsmiths' Hall, 1938

many examples are known, and it shows his supreme confidence and skill in bringing together the Arts and Crafts tradition with the stylised and dynamic modernism of the Art Deco era. All the rose bowls have this quality and yet all are subtly different in both form and decoration. Modernism and the Arts and Crafts Movement come together again in the coffee pot made for the Royal Academy of Arts, a piece in which contemporary elegance sits comfortably with a handcrafted finish.

In some commissions, Murphy was able to be an out and out modernist. A typical example is the casket presented to Fred Griffiths in 1931 by the partners of the Pioneer Works, Leamington Spa. Architectural in form, and enlivened by

Hand-raised casket with niello decoration, made in 1931 and presented to Fred Griffiths by his partners to celebrate the tenth anniversary of the Pioneer Works, Leamington Spa, 1921-1931

engraved panels, bands of stylised niello decoration and powerfully abstracted handles, this is in every sense a piece that reflects its period. The desk inkwell was another Murphy speciality, judging by surviving designs. However, not many may have been made. One that certainly was produced was that presented to the Orient Line, a distinctive design full of characteristic Murphy detailing that would have been in step with the Orient Line's well-known commitment to modernism. More conventional in terms of design but unusual in its decoration

Coffee pot in silver and ivory, presented to the Royal Academy of Arts by Richard Garbe, 1938

Hand raised salver made for the Port of London Authority and engraved with all the types of vessel associated with the Port of London, from drawings by Norman Wilkinson, the celebrated marine artist

is the salver for the Port of London Authority, with its engravings from drawings by the noted maritime artist, Norman Wilkinson, of many of the types of vessel to be seen in the Port of London. These drawings were probably engraved on to the salver by G.T. Friend, a craftsman who frequently worked in conjunction with Murphy and the Falcon Studio. It is thought this salver was destroyed by bombing during the Second World War.

Desk inkwell presented to the Orient Line
THE WORSHIPFUL COMPANY OF GOLDSMITHS

Watercolour design for the trophy for the Ladies High Diving Competition for the Southern Counties Amateur Swimming Association

CHAPTER 5

Sporting and School Trophies

In the 1930s the Murphy workshop made a policy of diversification, partly out of economic necessity and partly because of changes in the marketplace that reflected consumer demand. At the same time, Murphy himself was becoming a much more established figure through his increased standing in the Goldsmiths' Company, through his appointment as a Royal Designer for Industry, and through his involvement with the Central School of Arts and Crafts. This helped him to attract new clients and new kinds of work, for example for the corporate and civic market. Equally important was the move into the design and manufacture of sporting and educational trophies during a period when public interest in sporting activity was heightened by events such as the Berlin Olympic Games of 1936. Indeed, throughout the interwar years, and notably in the 1930s, the widespread enthusiasm for sport and athleticism was reflected by sculpture and the decorative arts in many parts of Europe.

A major source of inspiration in this field was the Goldsmiths' Company itself. In 1926 the Company organised the first of a series of competitions to improve the design of silver cups and trophies, as part of a broader Plate Improvement Scheme. Some of the impetus for this came indirectly from the King, who apparently was keen to see better designs for the three Ascot Cups. This first competition attracted ninety entries and was judged by the Director of the Victoria & Albert Museum, Sir Cecil Harcourt-Smith. Further competitions were held regularly until the outbreak of war and the King continued to see and approve the winning designs.

Murphy's productions include a series of classic sporting trophies in the form of standing cups and covers, notable for their blend of traditional eighteenth century elegance with contemporary Art Deco styling. A number of designs and sketches exist for these cups, which suggest that the latter element was initially more dominant. These are splendid and extravagant, and reflect Murphy's appreciation of both British and European Art Deco design details. In most cases the finished product was both simpler and more traditional, indicating both a sense of economy and a fear of the avant-garde on the part of his clients. Typical is his Ascot Royal Hunt Cup of 1938, an elegant but essentially traditional cup and cover cast in the classic mould of racing trophies. Only the finial hints at what might have been, had Murphy been given his head, while the handles use the conventional Art Deco styling familiar from silversmiths such as Harold Stabler. In this case, as in several others, the initial drawings and designs indicate a much more adventurous approach.

Elaborate designs also survive for the Duke of Gloucester Cup, a Shooting Trophy for Bisley. The actual trophy is again much simpler, but in this case a modern style was allowed to dominate, reflected by the fluted shape reminiscent, as in other Murphy pieces of this period, of the range of pottery designed by Keith Murray for Wedgwood. Other details underline Murphy's ongoing enthusiasm for contemporary Scandinavian and German silver, and his skill at blending engraving, piercing and modelling. A number of trophies follow this pattern, notably a cup and cover made for a medical school and a yachting trophy for the Upper Thames Sailing Club, the latter a simplified, yet more refined design brought to life by the pierced heron finial and stem. Another sailing trophy, known only from a design, combines similar modernist

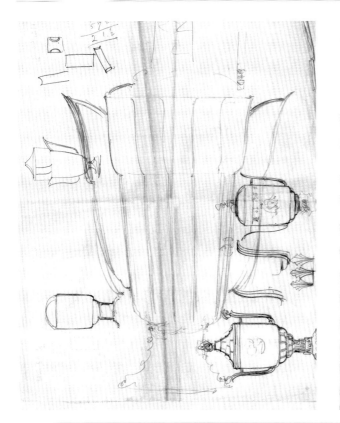

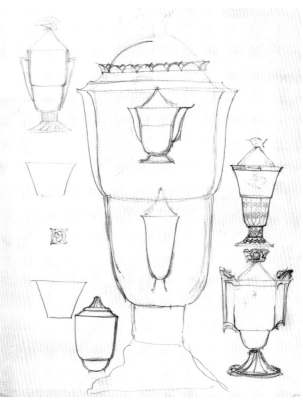

Pencil sketches for trophies, relating to the Royal Hunt Cup and the Duke of Gloucester Cup

Watercolour presentation design for the Royal Hunt Cup, 1938. Elaborate and expensive, and clearly modern in inspiration and detailing, this design was not used
THE WORSHIPFUL COMPANY OF GOLDSMITHS

Highly finished watercolour design for the Royal Hunt Cup. This simpler and more traditional design was accepted and noted accordingly 'approved but for silver.' The actual cup closely followed this scheme. Only the typical Murphy finial gives a hint of modernity

Presentation cup for a medical school, 1936, echoing the characteristic form and Art Deco detailing of the Duke of Gloucester Cup

engraving with an early chalice form. Judging by the attached order form from the Hatton Garden retailers, Lawn & Alder, this was also to be made in a series of miniatures, 3½in. high, presumably to be kept by the winners.

A similar arrangement was used for the series of cups made in the early 1930s for the Kandahar

Skiing Club. Murphy designed a number of Kandahar cups, each apparently accompanied by miniature versions. The design was initially quite conventional but it was made more exciting in 1934 by Art Deco detailing and large handles in the form of a letter K. More unusual, and more distinct in its Art Deco form, is the Duke of Kent

The Duke of Gloucester Cup, a shooting trophy for the National Rifle Association at Bisley, a classic Art Deco design in both shape and detailing

Full size sketch for a preliminary design for the Duke of Gloucester Cup, showing a more traditional, and more expensive approach. Unlike the Royal Hunt Cup, the approved design was in this case an improvement

THE WORSHIPFUL COMPANY OF GOLDSMITHS

Cup for the Kandahar Club. The cluster column style of the stem seems to echo a kind of mechanistic modernism but the source is probably rather different, for among the Murphy papers is a postcard showing a medieval Nottinghamshire font with a cluster column support.

The most consciously contemporary of all Murphy's trophies is that made for the RIBA Architects Golfing Society, whose modern vase shape is decorated with a delightfully drawn frieze of golfers, engraved by G.T. Friend. Similar in style is the National Physical Fitness Trophy, a low cup and cover whose twelve sides are

engraved with male and female figures symbolic of various sports. This was designed by Professor Gleadowe and made by Murphy in 1938, one of a group of pieces produced by that successful partnership that seem to reflect the spirit of their time.

As a commercial goldsmith with a large workshop to maintain, Murphy inevitably produced work of a more standard nature, in which the form was determined by the client. Typical is the Dr Cahill Trophy for the Irish Medical Golfing Society, a 2ft.6in. high replica in silver of a traditional Irish round tower. Also in

Heron Cup, commissioned by James Steel and presented by him to the Upper Thames Sailing Club, mid-1930s. Shown in the Exhibition of Modern Silverwork at Goldsmiths' Hall, 1938

Trophy for the Kandahar Skiing Club, 1935, a simple and stylish Art Deco form with a K finial

this category are two sailing trophies in the form of precisely detailed models of racing yachts or dinghies, one of which was commissioned in 1930 by Aleck Bourne for the United Hospitals Sailing Club. Such pieces reflect both the needs of the marketplace and the great skills of Murphy's workforce in the Falcon Studio.

The work produced by Murphy and the Falcon Studio specifically for schools and academies shows a similar blend of the conventional and the avant-garde. Notably conventional is the Edinburgh Academy rosewater dish commissioned by Lord Blanesburgh. Only the

pierced flower motifs and their zigzag borders reveal the actual date of the dish. Conventional in its inspiration but contemporary in its form and decoration is the ciborium-based Victor Ludorum Cup made in 1930 for Bromley High School for Girls. This was made by Murphy and presented by him to the school attended by his daughter, Pat. In 1935 she was runner-up in the school's senior sporting competition, and so nearly won her father's cup.

In 1934 Murphy presented another trophy to Bromley High School. This, a swimming award, was an altogether more adventurous design,

The National Physical Fitness Trophy, designed by Professor Gleadowe, engraved by G. Friend and made by Murphy, 1938. Shown at the Exhibition of Modern Silverwork at Goldsmiths' Hall in 1938, and made for presentation at the exhibition to the National Physical Fitness Council. It was returned to Goldsmiths' Hall during the Second World War

THE WORSHIPFUL COMPANY OF GOLDSMITHS

K handled version of the Challenge Cup for the Kandahar Skiing Club, 1934

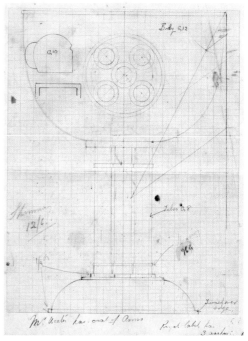

Measured drawing for the Duke of Kent Cup for the Kandahar Skiing Club

Large and small versions of the Duke of Kent Cup for the Kandahar Skiing Club, showing the distinctive shape and handles and the cluster-column stem

Trophy made for the Royal Institute of British Architects' Golfing Society, with a frieze of golfers engraved by George Friend, the most modern of all Murphy's sporting trophies

Scale drawing for the frieze of golfers, initialled by Friend

147

Racing trophy in the form of a dinghy, commissioned by Aleck Bourne in 1930 and presented to the United Hospitals Sailing Club

Dr Cahill Trophy for the Irish Medical Golfing Society, in a style echoing 19th century architectural forms

featuring a pierced roundel supported by fish and containing an Esther Williams-like figure swimming through stylised Art Deco waves beneath sunbeams. In style it is close to the series of pierced animal and zodiac brooches of the same period. Murphy clearly liked this design for he made at least two other versions of it. One, for the Ladies High Diving Competition of the Southern Counties Amateur Swimming Association, featured a similar roundel with athletic figures of lady swimmers diving through sunbeams. In the other, made for the swimming club of Rowntree's, the York-based confectionery manufacturer, the same roundel contains figures involved in various aquatic pursuits.

The Murphy archive contains photographs and designs for a number of other pieces with sporting and academic associations. These include a shield for the Essex Schools Tennis league, a rather old-fashioned Arts and Crafts object with

Rosewater dish commissioned by Lord Blanesburgh and presented to Edinburgh Academy

The Senior Victor Ludorum Cup, made by Murphy in 1930 and presented by him to Bromley High School for Girls, Kent

Georgina Clark, the school champion in 1935, holds the Victor Ludorum cup and shakes hands with the runner up, Pat Murphy, Harry's daughter

echoes of Voysey. Similar is a shield for the Dorset branch of the Royal Society for the Protection of Birds. Another shield-type award is a boys' school choir panel for the Hampstead and Hendon Musical Competition Festival, featuring a figure derived probably from stained glass. There is also a detailed design for a medal for the London Business Houses Amateur Sports Association, in a classical style with hints of 1930s athleticism, and a preliminary sketch of figures for a proposed

Swimming trophy made for Bromley High School for Girls and presented to the school by Murphy in 1934

Watercolour design for the trophy for the Ladies High Diving Competition for the Southern Counties Amateur Swimming Association, about 1935

Watercolour sketch for the Bromley High School swimming trophy

netball trophy. There is no indication that either of these was produced.

Competitions always appealed to Murphy and among the family papers are a number of competition designs, the majority of which were

County of Dorset Challenge Shield for the Royal Society for the Protection of Birds, 1933

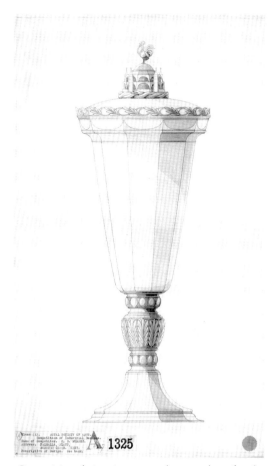

Competition design in pen and watercolour for the Swiney Cup prize in the Competition of Industrial Designs, the Royal Society of Arts. Undated, but probably early 1930s, and not produced although the basic form was used for other trophies

Watercolour design for a medal for the London Business Houses Amateur Sports Association, 1930s. There is no record of this medal being made

probably never produced. Typical is his finely detailed drawing for a trophy for the Swiney Cup Prize, entered into the Competition of Industrial Designs organised by the Royal Society of Arts. This brings together many of Murphy's favourite motifs, including a classical shape, Arts and Crafts and Art Deco detailing, and a symbolic architectural finial encompassed by a snake and surmounted by a crowing cockerel. The building has echoes of the old Wembley Stadium.

Ciborium in silver and ivory, mounted with gems, made for All Saints Church, Evesham, Worcestershire, 1936

CHAPTER 6

Ecclesiastical Work

In a period of significant change and development in architecture with the emphasis inevitably on domestic, commercial and industrial buildings, it is easy to overlook churches. However, new church building was also important during the 1920s and 1930s. In the ten years between 1926 and 1936 the Incorporated Church Building Society supported directly the planning and construction of over a hundred new churches in Britain, in both traditional and modern styles. Many major architects were involved in these schemes, including H.S. Goodhart-Rendel, Edward Maufe, Sir Giles Gilbert Scott, Sir Charles Nicholson, S.D. Adshead, W. Curtis Green, F. Gordon Troup and J.E. Newberry. Many other churches and religious buildings of different faiths were also constructed during this period with the help of the diocese, the parish and various forms of public, corporate and private sponsorship.

As a result, this period also witnessed a considerable demand for church fittings, notably woodwork, stone carving, metalwork, stained glass and textiles. Much of this demand was satisfied by the traditional and long established suppliers, such as Watts and Company, the St Dunstan Society and the Wareham Guild. However, modernist churches required a more contemporary style of fitting and organisations such as Heal's Ecclesiastical Studio were set up specifically to cater for this taste. This studio offered a design and manufacturing service covering all kinds of church fittings, often working in conjunction with leading modernist architects, for example Edward Maufe. At the same time companies such as the Royal Doulton pottery and individuals such as the silversmith Omar Ramsden responded to the demands of the ecclesiastical market.

For the silversmith this market was particularly important and had indeed been so since the 1840s, when it had been revived on a national scale by designers such as A.W.N. Pugin and manufacturers such as Hardman and Company. The commissioning of new church plate was a phenomenon throughout the Victorian era, with many magnificent pieces in a diversity of traditional and modern styles being made for

Gold chalice in 16th century style, set with cabochon gems and pearls. Date unknown, probably 1920s, possibly a private commission from a family in the south of England and subsequently given to a convent in Worthing

churches old and new all over Britain and throughout the British Empire. At the end of the century, the Arts and Crafts Movement, with its emphasis on handcraftsmanship, brought a new impetus to the making of church plate, marked by the emergence of figures such as Ramsden and Henry Wilson and by the revival of traditional techniques such as casting, chasing and enamelling. After the First World War the more modernist styles began to predominate, without any diminution in the scale of the ecclesiastical market, and so many of the leading names of the

Watercolour design for a 16th century-style chalice in silver gilt, mounted with opals and other gems. Calculations in pencil suggest it was made, but the present location is not known

period were actively involved in the design and manufacture of church plate, including Harold Stabler, Frank Dobson, Eric Gill, Leslie Durbin, C.W. Gilbert, Bernard Cuzner, Bernard Instone, Professor Richard Gleadowe and, of course, Harry Murphy and the Falcon Studio.

Murphy's first experience of ecclesiastical work was during his time in Henry Wilson's workshop and certainly he learned from Wilson an appreciation of medieval and later church metalwork generally and early medieval enamelling in particular. By 1910 his skills were sufficiently developed to make the separation of his work from his master's virtually impossible. Murphy was also a great collector of source material and among the great variety still preserved among his papers are books and published images of medieval church metalwork. These range from the Carolingian era to the fourteenth century, but the emphasis is on the enamel reliquaries from the Limoges region and Rhenish and Mosen altar crosses. Mixed in with these are photographs of work by Wilson, showing their clear dependence upon medieval models. Most of these have indications of Murphy's involvement in their manufacture. Also present are photographs of covered cups and chalices from later medieval and Tudor periods. It is apparent from these that Murphy had a wide-ranging appreciation of medieval and later church metalwork and was familiar with the collections of the Victoria & Albert and other museums. Such an appreciation was, at the time, by no means universal, but it was strongly associated with the followers of the Arts and Crafts Movement.

It is not possible to identify with certainty Murphy's earliest ecclesiastical work as so few examples of his work, ecclesiastical or secular, can be dated before the First World War. However, there does appear to be a progressive development of ideas from simple Arts and Crafts-style forms, with hand-hammered finishes and decoration with cabochon gems, to more sophisticated styles echoing fourteenth century and later models. Typical of the latter is a chalice of late fifteenth century form, perhaps made as a

15th century-style chalice, and related watercolour design, made for All Hallows Church, Barking, East London, 1920s or early 1930s

Chalice made for Murphy's local church, St Mary the Virgin, St Mary's Platt, Kent, 1928

Highly finished watercolour design for a chalice, in a generic 17th century style, probably for presentation to a client

Sketches by Murphy exploring the forms of stems for chalices, revealing a blend of historical and contemporary Art Deco inspiration   THE WORSHIPFUL COMPANY OF GOLDSMITHS

Silver and gold chalice commissioned in 1933 by Captain Harry Crookshank MP and presented by him to Lincoln Cathedral in thanksgiving for the successful completion of the building's restoration. The presentation was reported in The Times *on 18 April 1933*

private commission incorporating some of the family jewels, along with a drawing for a similar chalice. Closely linked to this in style is the chalice made for All Hallows Church, Barking, East London. The watercolour design for this is remarkably similar, showing that the finished chalice was altered only in minor ways in the production process. Another watercolour of a

chalice of the same basic form reveals Murphy's developing interest in simpler historical styles, more relevant to the Art Deco era.

Gothic models remain important, but there is a move towards the plainer styles of the seventeenth and early eighteenth centuries. A pair of plain but elegant chalices made for Peterborough Cathedral are typical. By the mid-

Pair of large (15in.) chalices in an 18th century style, made for Peterborough Cathedral, early 1930s

1930s Murphy had begun to explore a more contemporary approach to design and a more adventurous use of materials. A drawing in a sketchbook at Goldsmiths' Hall reveals his more experimental approach to the design of stems, a process that culminates in the ciborium made for All Saints Church, Evesham. The surviving watercolour sketches for this indicate Murphy's

design process. In its form and its combination of materials, silver, gold, cornelian and ivory, this cup is entirely an Art Deco object.

Murphy's most famous chalice is the one presented to Lincoln Cathedral in 1933 by Captain Crookshank MP to celebrate the restoration of the building. In its complexity of form and decoration, and its combination of gold

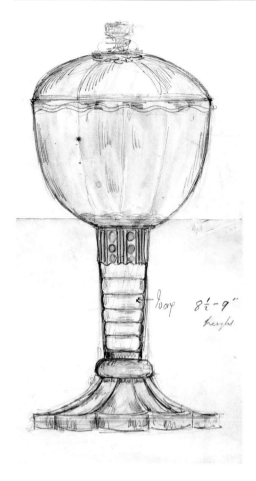

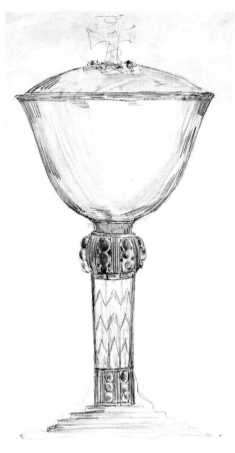

Preliminary pencil and watercolour sketches for the Evesham ciborium, showing stages in the development of the final design, and Murphy's confident way of applying Art Deco modernism to a traditional object. (See page 152)

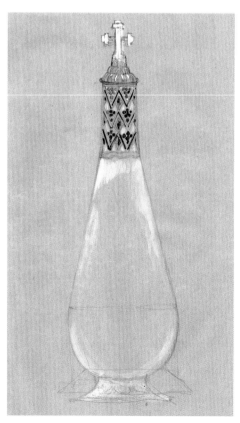

Pencil and watercolour designs for a flagon and oil vessel, to be made in glass mounted with silver and gold and set with gems, early 1930s

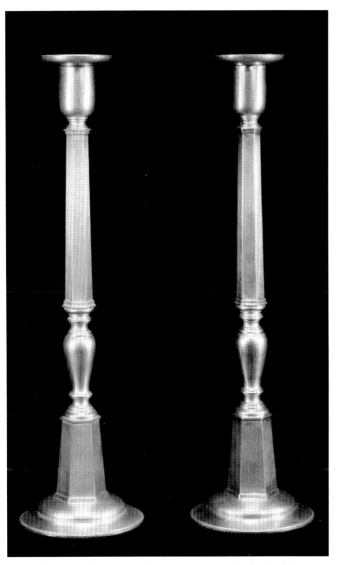

Pair of altar candlesticks and a monstrance made for St Mary Abchurch, in the City of London, 1930s. The monstrance is 28in. high

and silver, this brings together medieval, Byzantine and modern Art Deco styles. As such, it is a reflection of his growing confidence as a designer of ecclesiastical metalwork.

Murphy's ecclesiastical commissions were wide-ranging and highly varied. There are exciting watercolour designs for flagons and oil vessels, richly decorated in an almost Victorian

manner with gems and enamel, along with classically simple ewers and rosewater dishes, such as those made for Sidney Sussex College, Cambridge. This classical simplicity is also reflected by a monstrance, and the candlesticks made for St Mary Abchurch, in the City of London. Altar lamps and altar crosses were also in his repertoire, as shown by examples here dating

Altar cross in silver, made for St Cuthbert's Church, Darlington, 1930s. This striking Art Deco-style object, 26in. high, incorporates at its centre the traditional cross of St Cuthbert

Altar cross in brass, made for All Saints Church, Lichfield in 1922. This is one of the earliest examples of Murphy's ecclesiastical work, made at a time when he had no workshop or studio, and still carries echoes of the Arts and Crafts era

from the early 1920s in styles that are plainly historical in inspiration. A much more spectacular object is the silver altar cross made for St Cuthbert's Church, Darlington. While based entirely upon a historical model, this has the appearance, in its form and its decoration, of a totally contemporary object.

Throughout his career, Murphy was always ready to work with other designers, engravers, artists, silversmiths and architects, sometimes in a

creative partnership and sometimes as the maker of another's designs. A famous example of the latter was the gold and crystal communion set designed for St Paul's Cathedral by Sir Edwin Lutyens and made by Murphy. Consisting of three chalices, three patens and two flagons and completed in 1934, the set used the gold from an earlier service that had been discarded because it was 'ill-designed' and 'inartistic'. This new service echoed closely the styles of the sixteenth century,

Pencil design for a sanctuary or altar lamp, 1930s

with plenty of the kind of baroque details favoured by Lutyens. In order to perfect the chased and hammered style of decoration on the chalices, Murphy made first a full size replica in copper, which still survives in the family collection. Contemporary newspaper reports concentrated inevitably on Lutyens, with only passing references to 'Mr. H.G. Murphy, the craftsman', A similar relationship between architect and silversmith was that established by

Edward Maufe in his commissioning Murphy to supervise the design and production of a set of plate for Guildford Cathedral. Sadly, Murphy's death brought this to a close before anything had been produced.

Another example of artistic cooperation is the alms dish commissioned by the Goldsmiths' Company in 1930 from the sculptor and artist Eric Gill. This was made at the Royal College by E.B. Wilson, under Murphy's guidance, and bears

Set of gold and glass communion plate, designed by Sir Edwin Lutyens for St Paul's Cathedral, London, made by Murphy in 1934 and used for the first time at the Easter services in that year. According to a report in The Times in March 1934, the set was fashioned from the gold from the 19th century Canon Scott Holland memorial communion plate, a set rarely used because of its 'inartistic' design and impractical shape. Shown in the Exhibition of Modern Silverwork at Goldsmiths' Hall, 1938

Full size model of the St Paul's chalice made in copper by Murphy as a test piece for the shape and the engraving and chasing

Version of the Gill alms dish made by Murphy, 1930, with a changed rim and alterations to the balance and weight of the design

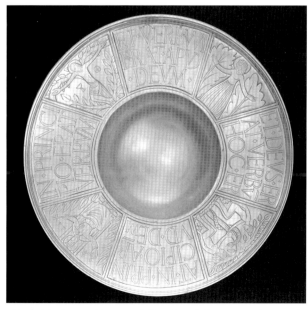

Alms dish designed by Eric Gill and made by E.B.Wilson at the Royal College of Art, London, 1930

the Falcon Studio mark. A second version was made by Murphy and engraved by Professor Gleadowe, with the addition of characteristic Murphy decoration around the rim.

Murphy's ecclesiastical work was an important part of his business, producing both financially rewarding commissions and considerable public status. The work is typical of the first decades of the twentieth century, reflecting as it does the transition from Victorian and Arts and Crafts revivalism to the more dynamic modernism of Art Deco. In this, it was entirely in step with the church building programme of the same period, equally divided between traditionalism and what Cecil Harcourt-Smith, chairman of the Incorporated Church Building Society and one-time Director of the Victoria & Albert Museum, called 'the modern school of thought'.

Appendices

Studio portrait photograph, 1930s

Harry Murphy was the ultimate master metalworker, supremely competent in the use and application of a wide range of decorative ornamentation. He learnt these ancient skills – repoussé, chasing, engraving, wire-work, gem setting, gilding, niello and enamelling in all its complex forms – from Henry Wilson, the greatest teacher of goldsmithing and silversmithing during the early years of the twentieth century.

After Murphy was appointed Head of Silversmithing at the Central School of Arts in 1932 he delivered numerous lectures to students, colleagues and faculties in Britain and in Europe. The following extracts, in Murphy's own words, reveal a craftsman in total command of his chosen discipline.

Enamel

Extract from an article on enamel (undated)

The true function of Enamel is surely the enrichment of a jewel, to give life and harmony of colour. To use as merely a splash of colour without design is a misuse of a very beautiful material. Is there anything more satisfying than a jewel set with stones and enriched with a careful arrangement of little patterns among the settings? It gives the ornament an interest that it otherwise would never have, and it possesses that quality of a Work of Art which improves on acquaintance, as it were, about which we can truly say "I am never tired of looking at this, there is always something fresh to be seen in it." How many diamonds and ornaments can that be said of?

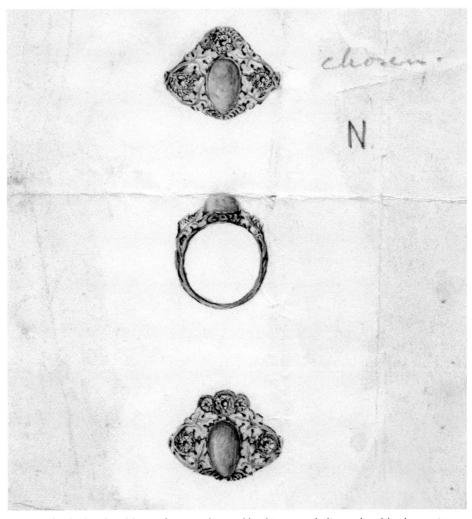

Designs for the bezel and hoop of a naturalistic gold, white enamel, diamond and hardstone ring

The following extracts are taken from a lecture delivered by Harry Murphy at Goldsmiths' Hall on 25 February 1935

Enamel is a glass compound of silver or flint with soda or potash. It is made by finely powdering the materials and subjecting them to white heat. The addition of oxide of lead in the glass makes it more refractive of light and at the same time more elastic and more easily fusible. Glass when cold is chemically very inert, so that hardly anything except hydrofluoric acid acts upon it, although when it is hot it has very powerful solvent qualities. By this means it may be coloured, for many metals are capable of imparting a characteristic colour to glass. Copper gives a turquoise blue; cobalt a royal blue; uranium a yellow, and chromium a green.

One of the most extraordinary properties of glass is the elasticity and strength it possesses when in thin sheets or threads. It can be spun as fine as hair and looks like floss silk. It is made into brushes and used in laboratories and in the jewellery trade for cleaning metal. If a very thin layer of metal be coated on each side with a thin layer of glass, the metal may be bent without the glass breaking. This extraordinary power of clinging to metal gives rise to the beautiful art of enamelling upon metals as practised by goldsmiths from remotest antiquity.

… Enamels are divided into three classes, and known by the French names champlevé, cloisonné, and plique-à-jour. The simplest form of enamelling, and probably the earliest known, was that which we understand by the term champlevé. The process is performed by cutting away a pattern on a thick piece of metal, leaving the outlines raised, then the parts cut away are filled in with enamels and fired, and then polished so that the whole pattern presents a uniform appearance. The degree of polish is, to my mind, as important as the scheme of colour, or design. Excessive polish gives a hard, glossy, tight, mechanical surface.

The process most nearly allied to champlevé is cloisonné. It differs only in this way: that the divisions or cloisons are made of strip of thin metal soldered to a metal ground.

… plique-a-jour is really similar to cloisonné, with this exception: that there is no metal background to the cloisonné. The design is either pierced out of metal or made up of wire, and then laid on mica, aluminium, bronze, or platinum, if you are wealthy. The work is then fired and, in cooling, leaves the mica, the effect being rather like a miniature stained-glass window. This is most suitable for ear-rings or head ornaments, though rather fragile. It is certainly not suitable for bowls and cups, which some misguided enthusiasts attempt.

… a cloak clasp done many years ago by Henry Wilson is in plique-à-jour. I do not see the point of plique-à-jour being used for that purpose; still, it was a very good job; very difficult to keep the drawing and at the same time enamel it so that it should be transparent.

… There is an enamel shield designed by Mr. Burridge and executed by Mr. Friend, the interesting point being that there is used in the background the basse-taille method of enamelling; that is to say, the ground is sunk down to a certain level and then it is carved into some form or other. The enamel is then flooded over, so that you get the depths giving the shadows in the drawing, the light of the higher portions giving the lighter shades.

… the most beautiful thing in the possession of the British nation is the gold cup in the British Museum known as the Kings' Cup, made by the process known as basse-taille. The whole of the figures are engraved below the surface and then flooded over with enamel; a most brilliant affair. I should advise all who have not already seen it to go to the British Museum and brood over this most wonderful example of the goldsmith's art. Nothing of the kind is done to-day. The colours are most beautiful, especially the reds. For some curious reason the blues have not only faded but the surface become dull, probably because of excess of borax in the enamel originally. The more borax there is in the enamel the less likely it is to withstand the atmosphere. For that reason most of the enamels done to-day will not last very long.

… In the next room you will see various modern products of industry; enamelled brush sets and articles of that description. You will see stampings of the backs before the brushes are prepared for enamelling. After they are stamped and shaped up they are engine-turned. Engine-turning produces the pattern which you see reflected through the enamel. It is done by a machine which is governed by the eccentric principle. It has a cutter which either revolves or goes up and down and then cuts and retreats, so that it is possible to make almost any number of designs desired. The enamel is then flooded over and there is produced what I call the basse-taille effect showing through. Enamel brush sets are very popular. I think they are the worst things one can possibly have. They are very thin; ladies use them in a hurry, drop them, and then they chip and have to be repaired. It seems to me a very improper use of the material but, for some reason or other, enamel brush sets seem to sell.

…There is some modern silver work designed by Miss Barnard and made by Barnard's of Hatton Garden; silver with enamel used on it; quite interesting from the point of view design, but I am not sure it is worth while doing much of, because if dropped it has to go back to the enameller's.

Murphy's direct, plain speaking manner obviously ruffled the feathers of several members of the audience as the following vote of thanks clearly testifies:

Mr. ALBERT CARTER; As President of the Birmingham Jewellers' and Silversmiths' Association, I thank Mr. Murphy very much for his interesting lecture, although I must say he has not been very complimentary to my side of the business. I can assure him that we have sold in this country during the last ten years probably £100,000 worth of enamel: that fearful stuff that breaks! We do repairs free of charge, and still we live! We guarantee that with ordinary wear and tear the enamel does not break and also that our enamel is made of the very finest material possible. It fires at 850 degrees F and the melting point of silver is just under 1,000 degrees F, so I can assure you it is real good enamel. I do not wish to criticise Mr Murphy. There are many things I can tell him about enamel that he does not know. Still, I thank him for his lecture: it has been very interesting, and I have great pleasure in moving a very hearty vote of thanks to him.

Bernard Instone, Murphy's fellow worker at Wilson's studio and colleague during his first unhappy stay in Germany then stood up and delivered a shining testimony on the excellent work of Albert Carter. By this time feelings were plainly running high since Murphy responded:

I am sure Mr. Albert Carter will forgive me if I have made any derogatory remarks about his work. I was not, of course, referring to the works of art we see in that respect. I was referring particularly to the shoddy pieces which, in so many ways, spoil the sale of the good stuff. You see them in little shops where auctions are held in Oxford Street and such places. I am not referring to Mr. Albert Carter's work. I know the enormous amount of research which has gone into it. It is absolutely a specialised work, and work which he has carried on for years, but that does not mean I am not entitled to my opinion as to what I feel about it. I daresay 90 per cent. of those present like it very much, and I am sure they are entitled to.

Murphy must have been feeling pretty beleaguered, as the next speaker, Mr. H. De Koningh, stood up to scoff at his appreciation of the King's Cup in the British Museum and heavily criticise his remarks about basse-taille enamelling. Perhaps unsurprisingly the meeting, at this point, was concluded.

APPENDIX 2

Niello

Extracts from Murphy's own working notes and a lecture delivered at Goldsmiths' Hall on 25 February 1935

The study of niello work carries us back to the subject of engraved designs in metals with which art is intimately connected. Such designs were at first used as finished ornamentation in themselves. Subsequently known specimens dating back to about the 1st century A.D. were treated with a further process, the engraved lines being filled up with a black metallic amalgam now known as niello.

The composition of niello is copper, silver, lead and flowers of sulphur. My own recipe is 3 parts silver, 2 parts copper and 1 part lead. The copper and silver are melted together in a crucible and when properly mixed the lead is added. The whole is stirred with a green stick and then poured into the flowers of sulphur. The lead gives brittleness to the copper and silver and the flowers of sulphur oxidizes the metal and gives it its characteristic black appearance. When nearly cold it is hammered into a thin plate and then remelted, hammered again and it is then ready for use. This usually involves taking a piece of silver on which is engraved the design or pattern required, coating it with borax and placing the niello over the pattern until it is entirely covered. It is then heated in a furnace which causes the niello to melt and fill up the interstices of the design. Finally, the piece of silver is rubbed smooth to reveal the black pattern

Silver jewellery and accessories with niello decoration

APPENDIX 3

Golds

Extract from a lecture given by Murphy (undated)

Within the past few years progress has been made in the production of articles in gold of two or more tints.

The colour effects are mainly produced by the addition of silver and copper. Thus an alloy containing 90% silver and 10% of gold is sold as white gold for gem setting. With about 25% silver gold assumes a greenish yellow tint and is known as green gold. Green gold was known to the ancients as electrum, a natural alloy of silver and gold.

The addition of copper considerably heightens the yellow colour of gold, the alloys passing through different shades of yellow to red yellow and finally to the rich red of copper as the proportion of copper is increased. By a suitable adjustment of the silver a number of grey alloys are also produced and by the addition of iron alloys with a blue tint are produced. The addition of palladium to gold has the effect of bleaching and the higher carats are alloyed this way.

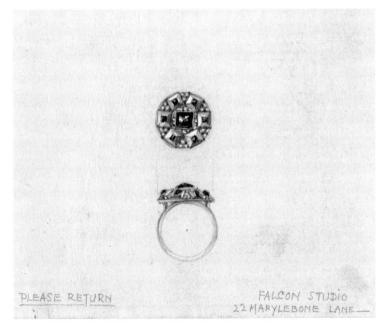

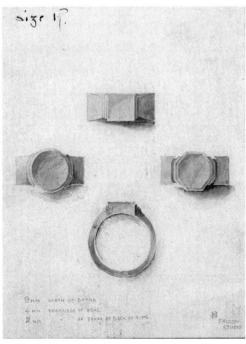

Designs for a diamond set gold ring and a gold signet ring

APPENDIX 4

Work of the School

Comments by Murphy concerning his role at the Central School of Arts and Crafts and written after 1935.

Every Principal of the Central School of Arts and Crafts has had his own personal contribution to make to its work. Each one under whom I have worked has enriched the tradition of the School in some way. Mr Burridge perfected the organisation of the School and brought it to a very high standard of efficiency. Mr Jowett was an ambassador for the School, and by his charm and grace of manner won recognition for it in a wider sphere, and left it with reputation and status enhanced.

I have definite views on what I consider should be the next step forward in the work of the School. As I see it, my contribution would be to bring the School into a more vital contact with the needs of Industry. I conceive the School as a unity – not divided into self-contained compartments, but an organic whole, charged with one vital force and purpose: to train students to meet the demands of industry and to

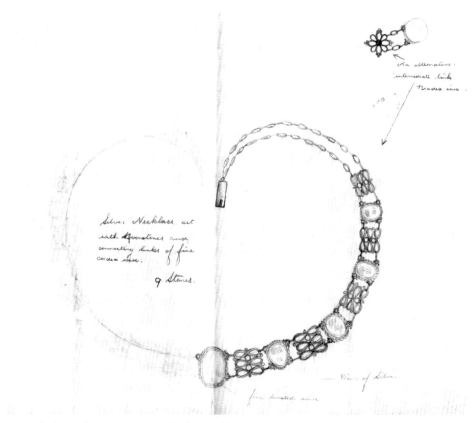

An early design for a moonstone and silver necklace. There are strong parallels between this piece and an enamelled gold necklace in the Renaissance style by Henry Wilson

170

bring them into touch with the people who can utilise their gifts and training.

Students come to the School with half-formed ideas about the work they want to do, and often they may elect to take classes in subjects for which they have no real aptitude. The consequence is that when they leave the School they have very indifferent prospects of making a success of their careers.

My aim would be to bring each student into touch with every Department of training in the School, so that his or her true bent would be revealed, both to the student and to the instructors. I should try to develop a system whereby students were given the opportunity of working together in co-operation. The designer and technician would be brought together to produce a complete article, each receiving stimulation from contact with a different type of brain and the intensified interest brought about by group activity.

The tendency today is for Art and Industry to become more and more closely connected. I believe that more emphasis than hitherto should be laid on instruction in craftsmanship and its application to industrial requirements. It would therefore be my aim to foster close relationship with manufacturers, to bring the work of the School and its students continually to their attention, so that there may always be position available for students in industrial life when they pass out of school. This, I claim, would be the final proof of efficient training.

APPENDIX 5

Employees and Assistants at the Falcon Studio

An emerald and gold parure by Leslie Woodard exhibiting the strong influence of Harry Murphy in its design and construction

Records of Murphy's employees, assistants and apprentices at his various workshops are incomplete. However, the following names are known: Mr Aspley, Peter C. Cook, Leslie Durbin, Louis Galvin, Sidney Hammond, Terence John Lawrence, Mr Massey, Richard Simmonds and Leslie Woodard. Murphy also worked closely with colleagues at the Central School of Arts and Crafts and the Royal College of Art. In addition he often worked in partnership with established designers, artists, architects, engravers and other specialised craftsmen, notably Professor Richard Gleadowe, George Friend, Eric Gill, Sir Edwin Lutyens, Edward Maufe and Professor Richard Garbe.

Designs for Jewellery: 1926-38

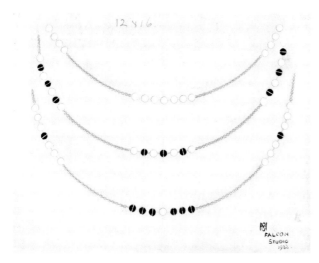

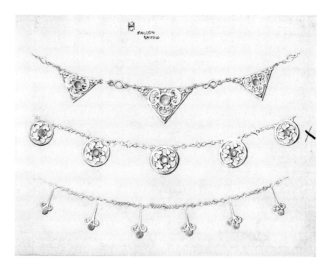

Gem set chains and necklaces

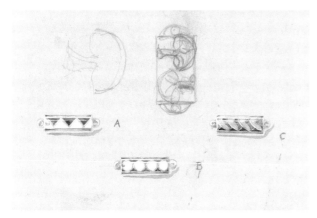

Clasps for necklaces and beads

Brooches

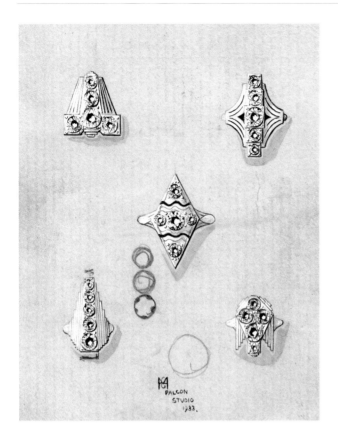

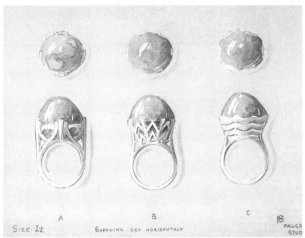

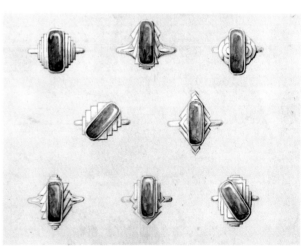

Falcon Studio designs for rings. By the mid-1930s Murphy had fully embraced the spare lines and architectural symmetry which typified the Art Deco era

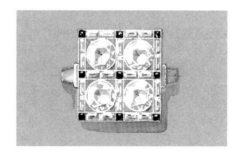

Five various designs for an amethyst and pearl naturalistic pendant.

Designs for Accessories: 1930–38

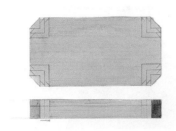

Compacts

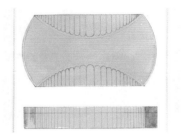

Cigarette cases

Vanity case

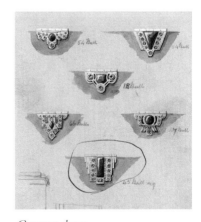

Compact clasps

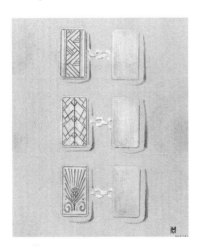

Cufflinks

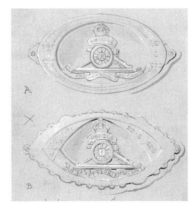

Regimental insignia

Black Ink Drawings: Designs for Silver Figurative Brooches, Engraved Details and Finials

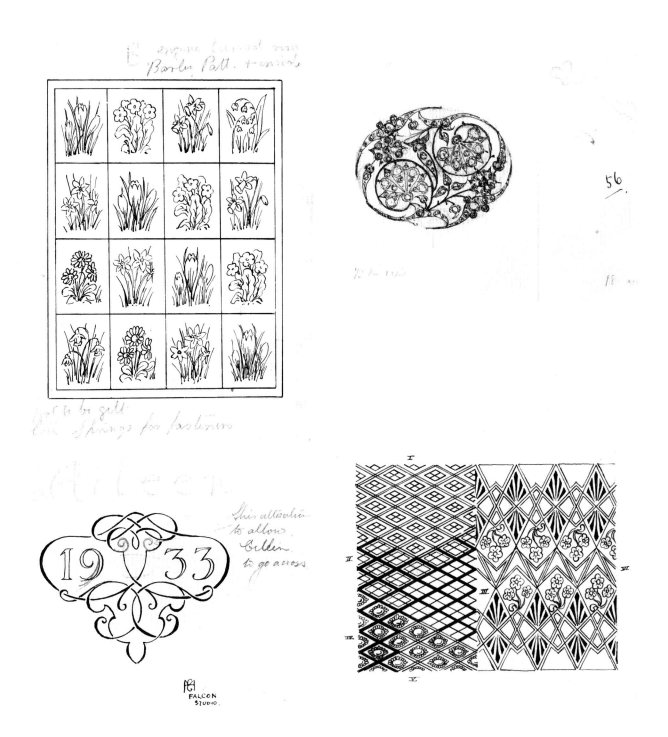

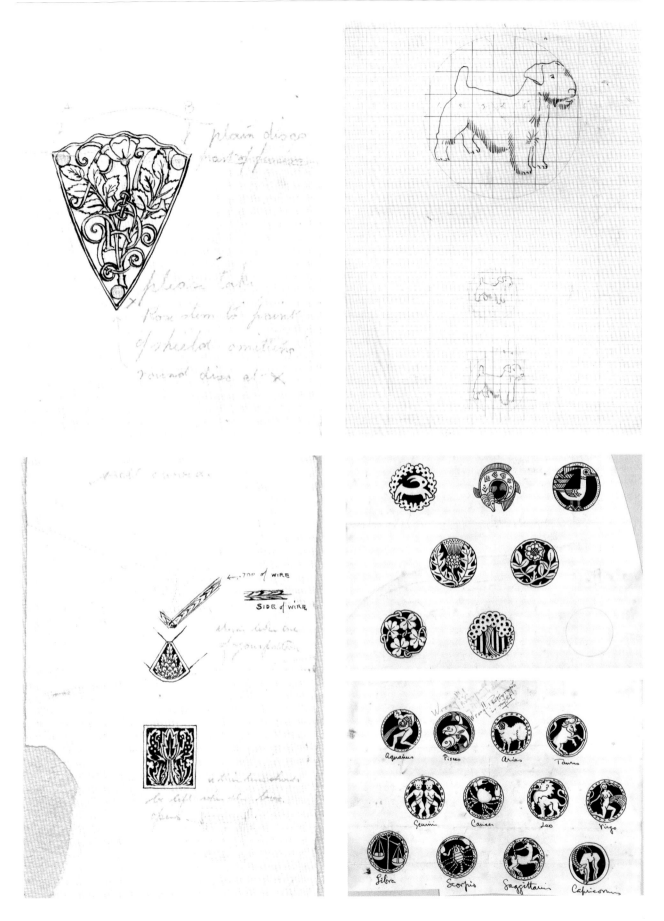

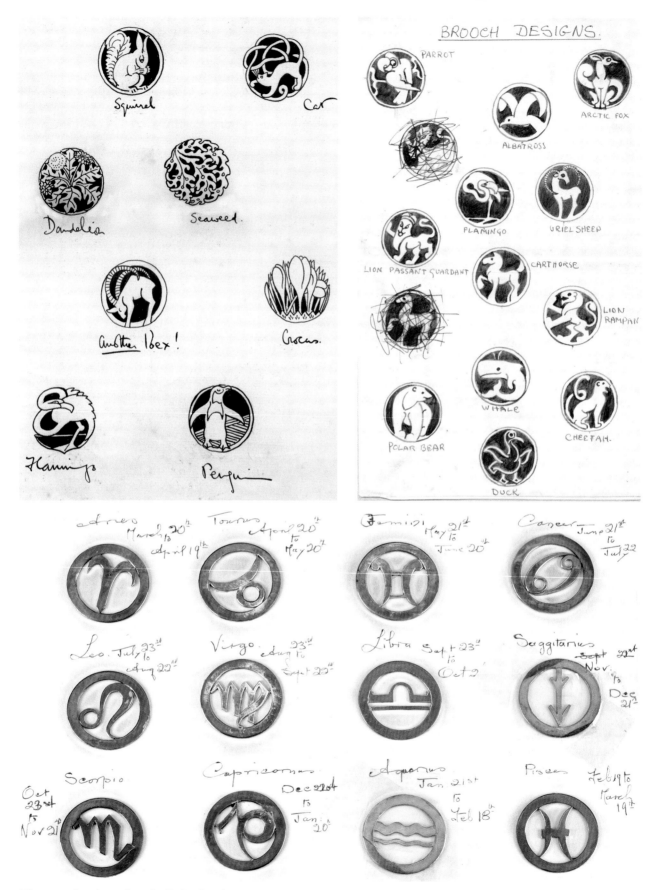

The original steel templates for Zodiac brooches

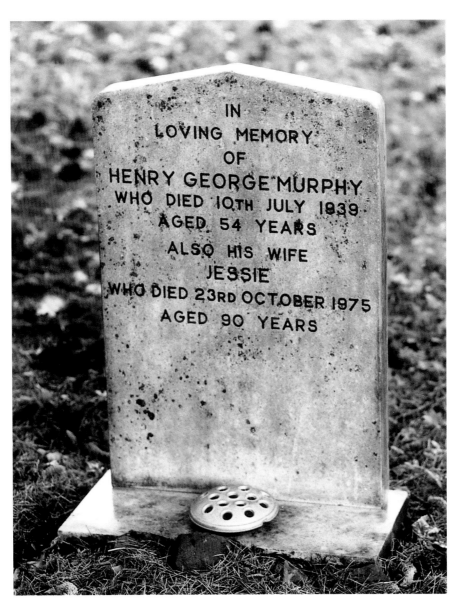

Harry and Jessie Murphy are buried side by side at the Church of Mary the Virgin, St. Mary's Platt, Kent

INDEX

Page numbers in bold type refer to illustrations and captions